WHERE THEY LIVED IN LONDON

Maurice Rickards

WHERE THEY LIVED IN LONDON

DAVID & CHARLES

© MAURICE RICKARDS 1972

ISBN 0 7153 5259 8

Designed by Maurice Rickards

Set in 9/11 pt Times
and printed in Great Britain
by Clarke Doble & Brendon Limited   Plymouth   Devon
for David & Charles (Publishers) Limited
South Devon House   Newton Abbot   Devon

INTRODUCTION

AS EVERY LONDONOLOGIST KNOWS, this city can be enjoyed twice over: once for what it is and once again for what it was. The evidence of what it was is everywhere; scattered among the building and rebuilding it appears as a unifying framework—the basic structure on which the new is superimposed. With its mews and terraces, its squares and side-streets, its railings and fanlights, what it was is no less real than the glass and ferro-concrete of today. It serves not only as a reminder of the past but as a frame and foil for the present. Sometimes it shines with special brightness.

Consider an undistinguished house in the Lambeth Road—the spit and image of its neighbours. It becomes spectacularly transformed by the knowledge that 'William Bligh, Commander of the *Bounty*, lived here'. This little house (not the one to the right or the left, but this particular house) was Bligh's home. He set foot upon its threshold, talked and walked in it, peered down from its windows, whistled in its garden . . . The effect on the beholder, whatever his verdict on the man, is magical. Number 100 Lambeth Road gains not merely distinction but an almost visible aura.

London provides a wealth of opportunity for such magic. This capital city, in constant daily use for upwards of nineteen hundred years, has amassed so much in the way of historical association that it would be hard to find a patch that is free of it. Among its aggregate of many millions it counts more celebrities per acre than perhaps any other city in the world. As natural-born inhabitants, as haven-seekers, as prospectors, adventurers or passing philosophers; as rogues, reformers, performers and straightforward tourists, it has at one time or another sheltered virtually everybody who is, or was, anybody.

In some areas celebrities have lived so thick and fast it seems they must have jostled each other on the pavement. Consider, for example, Frith Street, Soho. Scarcely more than two hundred yards long, this apparently undistinguished street has distinction at every hand. As well as William Hazlitt and John Logie Baird (featured here on pages 22 and 24) its residents and habitués have included Mozart, Samuel Coleridge, Edmund Kean, Lord Macaulay, Sheridan and Macready, Chopin and Mendelssohn, Vincent Novello the publisher and His Excellency the Venetian Ambassador.

Consider neighbouring Greek Street and Dean Street. These between them claim, as well as Karl Marx (page 20), Thomas de Quincey, Giovanni Casanova, Josiah Wedgwood, Dougles Jerrold, Dr Arnold, Sir James Thornhill, Mrs Thrale, Joseph Nollekens, Lucia Bartolozzi and Theodore, King of Corsica. Close by—all within sedan-chair distance—are the addresses of Jean Paul Marat and Thomas Rowlandson (both in Romilly Street), Edmund Burke and John Dryden (both Gerrard Street) and Thomas Sheraton (Wardour Street).

Soho is not alone in its historicity. Open the file on any area—virtually any street—in London, and names fall out six or seven at a time. It is almost an embarrassment of glory. Much of the glory—but by no means all of it—is marked by commemorative plaques. For the thoughtful stroller these serve as instant time machines—restoring yesterday at a glance. With only the smallest effort of the imagination the eye strips the scene of today's impedimenta and sees the building as it was in former days.

But here a word of caution: even the wisest stroller sometimes overlooks an element of change that must affect his assessment—the change in relative location that the growth of London has brought about. As the outskirts of today move out, those of yesterday appear to move in.

When Thomas Carlyle moved to London from his rural Craigenputtock he sought the advantages of the big city, but he sought solitude as well. The house at Cheyne Row, though well served by the horse omnibus, was in a secluded, almost rural, quarter of the town. He wrote to his wife, after viewing the house for the first time, 'We lie safe at a bend of the river, away from all the great roads; we have air and quiet hardly inferior to Craigenputtock, an outlook from the back windows into mere leafy regions with here and there a red high-peaked old roof looking through; and see nothing of London except by day the summits of St Paul's Cathedral and Westminster Abbey . . .' But the great roads were soon to catch up with him. Close by the house today a six-lane highway flanks the river bend.

To the north, not long before Carlyle moved in to Cheyne Row, William Hazlitt was stumping the steets in the area of Oxford Street—at that time close to the northern limits of the town.

The 'Oxford Road' had for centuries formed a boundary line. South were the new-built streets and squares that had appeared in the years following the Great Fire; to the north was a doubtful countryside, a leafy haunt of footpads and highwaymen. Even in 1830, Hazlitt's house off Soho Square was within half a mile of open country.

Thirty years earlier, when William Blake was living at South Molton Street and Lord Nelson was in lodgings at New Bond Street, the Oxford Road was still just climbing into respectability. Though building was under way along its south side, it was still possible, as late as 1760, to pick blackberries in the hedgerow along its 'rural' side. The historian Pennant reports that the road was rutted deep and hollow—'full of sloughs, with here and there a ragged house, the lurking-place of cut-throats . . . I was never taken that way by night (in my hackney coach to a worthy uncle's who gave me lodgings at his house in George Street) but I went in dread the whole way.'

While blackberries grew in Oxford Street, Mozart's Ebury Street, then Five Fields Row (page 94), was well outside the town. This area too was known for its hazards. 'The Fields,' says one report, 'were the terror of foot-passengers proceeding from London to Chelsea after nightfall.'

For the few who spent any time in these parts (including Mozart senior, who was trying to recover from a sore throat) there was a further hazard: the swampy humours of its marshes made it inadvisable to breathe too deep.

The westward progress of the town for all practical purposes stopped short at the western end of Piccadilly. (The Duke of Wellington's house at Hyde Park Corner was for long nick-named 'No 1, London'.) The villages of Chelsea, Battersea, Kilburn,

Camden Town and Paddington were scarcely more than hamlets. As Keats well knew, Hampstead was a jolting coach-ride out of town and up the hill—an hour and a half in good weather.

Useful though it is, the commemorative plaque takes no account of the tide of local change. The observer reminds himself of the obvious fact that there was no betting shop in William Blake's South Molton Street, and of the less obvious one that the street itself was close to the sight and sound of country farmyards.

The Blue Plaque (now well over the three hundred mark) copes with an ever-increasing press of history. It is just managing to hold its own. It was in July 1863 that William Ewart sought the opinion of the House of Commons as to whether 'it might be practical . . . to have inscribed on the houses in London which have been inhabited by celebrated persons, the names of such persons'. (He was destined, a century later, to be the subject of such an inscription himself; his plaque—*William Ewart, Reformer*—is at 16 Eaton Place.) Mr Cowper, First Commissioner of Public Works, welcomed the idea, but cautioned that 'it might not be desirable to compel a man to place upon his house the name of a person who did not then live there'. There was also the difficulty that present occupiers might prefer people not to know how old their houses were. The idea would, however, be looked into.

It was the Royal Society of Arts that looked into it. On 7 May 1866 the first of the Society's plaques went up on Byron's house in Holles Street. (The house is now demolished, but the shop window of the John Lewis Partnership, whose building now occupies the site, carries its own reminder.) By the turn of the century the Society had put up some thirty further tablets; in 1903, when the Society handed the scheme over to the London County Council, the full count stood at thirty-six. There had been no compulsion, and few objections. Though many of the original houses, like Byron's, have since been demolished, several of the Society's original tablets still remain.

By the early 1970s the London County Council and its successor, the Greater London Council, between them had put up some 370 tablets. Demolition has reduced the total of some 400 to today's 322. New plaques appear at a rate of some half-a-dozen a year.

Newcomers are added, not by autocratic nomination of the Greater London Council, but as a result of proposals from the public. Criteria of eligibility are rigidly observed: twenty years must have elapsed since the subject's death; he must be recognised as eminent in his own field; he must have made 'some important positive contribution to human welfare or happiness' and he must be a familiar name to the ordinary man of the next generation.

Not all subjects prove universally popular. Karl Marx caused some rumblings; so did Oscar Wilde. Marie Stopes' blue plaque, though similar to the 'official' design, is in fact non-municipal; it was put up independently by private subscription.

This book offers a cross-section of London's famous names and addresses, some plaque-bearing, some not. The majority are within a mile or so of Piccadilly Circus.

They appear as a series of five 'neighbourhoods' or sections; (the committed pilgrim may stroll conveniently from point to point—perhaps on an idle Sunday afternoon; the less committed may settle for an idle Sunday armchair). The last section comprises addresses too scattered for a combined visit, but of which perhaps one or two may merit a special sortie on their own.

In only four cases, those of Dickens, Keats, Carlyle and Dr Johnson, are the houses open to the public. These, maintained with loving care by full-time custodians, also house relics and memorabilia of their former occupants. For the rest the buildings continue to serve their function as private premises—part of the ordinary scene of London's daily life. Indeed, all of the buildings shown in the pictures are photographed not as monuments or as subjects for photo-idyllics, but as items of every day—delivery vans, parking meters, litterbins and all.

Each picture shows an original building, substantially unchanged since the time of its famous occupant. Give or take a growth of ivy or a window-box or two, each is much as it was. Only in a few cases, where former private houses now appear with shop fronts, have changes been spectacular. In only two cases, those of Thomas Gains-borough (page 44) and Lord Lister (page 60) have interior alterations materially changed the layout of the buildings.

At the back of the book there is a list of additional notable names and addresses. These, for the truly dedicated, represent further possible pilgrimages. As with those in the body of the book, the addresses are all of original buildings. All are within easy reach of Central London.

The list is drawn largely from the booklet *Blue Plaques*, the Greater London Council's full directory of houses bearing plaques erected under Council auspices. It will be remembered however that plaques are put up by other agencies, public and private. The City Corporation has over 120 in the City of London, and private initiative has been responsible for a fair number. As well as Marie Stopes' plaque (Whitfield Street), those for Bernard Shaw (Fitzroy Square) and Anna Pavlova (North End Road) have been put up independently. Some buildings, like Winston Churchill's house at Hyde Park Gate, carry no plaque at all.

The book is dedicated to those for whom, plaque or no plaque, some houses have an almost visible aura.

MAURICE RICKARDS

Fitzroy Square, July 1971

INDEX OF NAMES

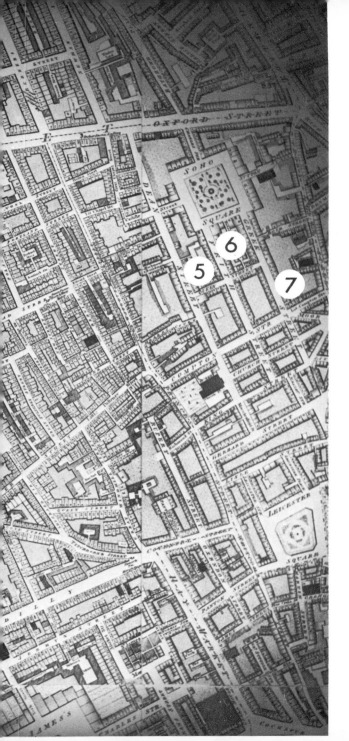

MAYFAIR/SOHO AREA

(Within 1 mile of Piccadilly Circus)

The map shows London in 1792 (roughly as it was in Nelson's time). The basic layout is the same as that of today, but there are important differences in detail. Charing Cross Road has not yet arrived, nor have Regent Street, Piccadilly Circus, Shaftesbury Avenue, and other landmarks. The map, like those on other pages, may be taken only as a general guide to locations.

WILLIAM BLAKE (1757–1827)

17 South Molton Street W1

Blake claimed to have seen visions from an early age. When he was only eight or ten years old he said he saw a tree filled with angels on Peckham Rye. But he was not without an understanding of worldly affairs and was punctilious in money matters. From South Molton Street he wrote to William Hayley: 'I have regularly written down every sum I have receiv'd from you; & tho' I never can balance the account of obligations with you I ought to do my best in all circumstances. I find that you was right in supposing that I had been paid for all I have done; but when I wrote last requesting ten pounds, I thought it was due but I did not advert to the Twelve Guineas which you lent me . . . I am therefore 12 Guineas in your Debt . . .'

ROBERT SOUTHEY, WHO VISITED BLAKE here in 1811, thought he was insane. Samuel Palmer, who knew him intimately, described him as 'the most practically sane, steady, frugal and industrious' man he had ever met. Blake was certainly no ordinary man.

When he moved in at South Molton Street in October 1803 he was under the threat of imprisonment. In Felpham, where he had been living previously, he had forcibly ejected a soldier from his cottage garden and by way of revenge the soldier had charged him with sedition. The trial took place at Chichester in January 1804, and 'to the uproar and noisy exultations' of the public gallery, Blake was acquitted.

He returned to his two rooms on the first floor at South Molton Street and took up again where he had left off with his visions.

Of his 'Jerusalem', which was issued not long after his arrival here, he wrote 'I have written this poem from immediate dictation, twelve, or sometimes twenty or thirty lines at a time without premeditation, and sometimes even against my will.' He spoke of it as 'the grandest poem that this world contains'. The work was not really his, he said: 'I may praise it since I dare not pretend to be any other than the secretary—the authors are in eternity.'

Among his many visionary portrait sitters, all of them painted in spiritual visits to South Molton Street, were Moses, Julius Caesar, Solomon, the builder of the pyramid, Mary and Joseph, and Mohammed. He painted these portraits 'looking up from time to time as though there were a real sitter before him'. His wife Catherine, illiterate daughter of a Battersea market gardener, also saw visions. She also learnt to paint. Often at night 'when he was under his very fierce inspirations' she would get up with him while he yielded himself to the muse 'to sit motionless and silent . . . without moving hand or foot; this for hours, and night after night.'

Blake was not happy here. Apart from the patronage and care of a few friends, society largely ignored him. He put on a one-man show in a room above his brother's hosiery shop in Broad Street, but hardly anyone came. When some of his drawings were shown to George III, His Majesty looked at them for a while and then said, 'Take them away'. In 1957 a bust of the artist was unveiled in Poets' Corner, Westminster Abbey.

Underground Station:
BOND STREET

12

When application was made in October 1967 to allow a licence for the use of part of 17 South Molton Street as a betting shop over two dozen residents signed a protest and there were strong objections from Sir Geoffrey Keynes, secretary of the Blake Trust. In a letter to 'The Times' a director of a South Molton Street firm wrote 'Can you imagine the Soviet government allowing the homes of say Tolstoy or Dostoyevski, where much of their great work was undertaken, to be turned into betting shops? Would the Germans likewise treat the homes of Goethe, Mozart or Bach? But our Inner London Sessions Appeals Committee thought otherwise in respect of William Blake.'

Like most of the other buildings in the area, this was originally a private house with living rooms on the ground floor. The picture shows the house as it was when Handel first rented it (£35 a year and 17s 6d [87½p] rates) in 1724. On Handel's death in 1759 his janitor, John De Bourke, bought the house with the whole of its contents and set it up as lodgings.

GEORGE FREDERICK HANDEL (1685–1759)   25 Brook Street W1

Good eating was Handel's only luxury. All else at Brook Street was of an almost spartan simplicity. When he died the entire contents of the house, appraised by independent valuers, was worth £48. But his personal fortune amounted to over £17,500.

THIS WAS HANDEL'S ADDRESS for thirty-five years. A naturalised Englishman who remained permanently incapable of mastering the language, he was the brightest jewel in Britain's musical crown. Born Georg Friedrich Haendel, at Halle in Lower Saxony, he visited London on leave of absence from his post as Kapellmeister to the Elector of Hanover; as it turned out he went down so well with the British—and they with him—that he overstayed his leave and finally stayed for good. He was disconcerted when his erstwhile employer (equally bad at English) became King George I of England; there was some question as to whether Handel should emerge from his Brook Street home to look the new monarch in the eye. However, that turned out all right too: the king granted him a salary of £400 a year. The king's son George II did even better; at a performance of *Messiah* he was so moved by the opening of the Hallelujah Chorus that he rose to his feet and remained standing till the end; the audience rose too, and has been doing so at this point ever since.

From Brook Street Handel strolled out into the streets of London—'a familiar, lumbering figure . . . He prowled through the streets . . . *browsed* through them . . .' He ambled up to Grosvenor Square or to see Sir Hans Sloane, at whose house, on a disastrous occasion, he rested a hot buttered muffin on the binding of one of his host's library volumes. ('To be sure it was a careless trick,' conceded Handel, 'but it did no monstrous mischief; yet it put the old bookworm terribly out of sorts. I offered my best apologies, but the old miser would not have done with it.')

In the house at Brook Street in just twenty-four days he composed *Messiah*. His biographer, Newman Flower, recounts:

'He did not leave the house. His manservant brought him food, and as often as not returned in an hour to the room to find the food untouched, and his master staring into vacancy. When he had completed part II, with the *Hallelujah Chorus*, his servant found him at the table, tears streaming from his eyes. "I did think I did see all heaven before me, and the great God himself!" he exclaimed.'

Apart from music, Handel's other interests were children (he was a Governor of the Foundling Hospital in Mecklenbergh Square) and food and drink. On one occasion, when a friend dined with him at Brook Street, he was discovered to have left the table to drink privately in another room.

Underground Station:
BOND STREET

HORATIO NELSON (1758–1805)

103 New Bond Street W1

An onlooker at Dresden (1800) described Nelson as 'one of the most insignificant figures I ever saw in my life'. His weight could not be more than seventy pounds, 'and a more miserable collection of bones and wizened frame I have never yet come across . . .' He was 'almost covered' with orders and stars.

NELSON WAS THIRTY-NINE WHEN he lodged here in 1798. He was home on leave. There had been ten major engagements, culminating in the disaster at Santa Cruz. Still to come were eight more years to live, the Nile, Copenhagen and Trafalgar. He was recovering from the amputation of his right arm, which had been shattered in the action at Tenerife.

'His sufferings . . . were long and painful,' says Southey. 'A nerve had been taken up in one of the ligatures at the time of the operation; and the . . . ends of the ligature being pulled every day, in hopes of bringing it away, occasioned fresh agony.'

'Lady Nelson . . . attended the dressing of his arm until she had acquired sufficient resolution and skill to dress it herself. One night . . . after a day of constant pain, Nelson retired early to bed, in the hope of enjoying some respite by means of laudanum . . .' London that evening was bright with the celebration of Duncan's victory over the Dutch at Camperdown; Nelson had not been in bed long before crowds came, violently knocking at the door, and wanting to know why there were no celebration lights in the windows. A servant explained that Nelson was inside, asleep. 'The feeling of respect and sympathy was communicated from one to another with such effect, that . . . the house was not molested again.' Nelson was already immortal.

In a few weeks he had sufficiently recovered to send a message up the road to St George's, Hanover Square: '*An officer desires to return thanks to Almighty God . . .*'

It was later in the same year, in Naples, that Nelson met Lady Hamilton, the servant girl from Cheshire who had become the wife of the British envoy to the Neapolitan court, and who in 1801 became the mother of a daughter called Horatia.

Emma, Lady Hamilton, dominated Nelson. London society was amazed at his submission: 'She leads him about like a keeper with a bear,' wrote a friend; 'She must sit by his side at dinner to cut his meat and he carries her pocket handkerchief.'

Her husband, Sir William, was charmed with Nelson; in his will he left him a picture of his wife, 'a small token of the great regard I have for his lordship, the most virtuous, loyal and truly brave character I have ever met with'. Sir William died in Emma's arms, her hand and Nelson's clutched in his.

Underground Station:
BOND STREET

The records show some ten or eleven London addresses for Nelson between 1783 and 1805— most of them 'short-stay' addresses and most of them, it may be observed, not far from the Hamiltons' house in Piccadilly (below). *No 103 New Bond Street (right) to which the text refers, is the only original Nelson residence that remains.* Nelson also stayed at a house on the site of No 147 New Bond Street but this has since been rebuilt.

ANTONIO CANAL
(CANALETTO) (1697–1768) 41 Beak Street W1

Canaletto's Venetian vision followed him everywhere. This detail is from his painting of the Thames as he saw it in the year 1747.

IT WOULD NOT BE TOO MUCH TO SAY that Canaletto's success as a painter stemmed from the demands of the tourist trade. When he was twenty-three Canaletto returned to his native Venice from his apprenticeship in Rome. He had started as a theatrical scene painter in the studio of his father, but Rome had changed his mind: in Venice he set up as a 'view painter' —a one-man forerunner of the picture postcard industry.

The tourist in Venice, particularly the English tourist, wanted to bring back with him pictorial evidence of his trip abroad. Canaletto, having formulated an approach to view-painting which combined accuracy with pictorial sensitivity, obliged. His formula, adopted early in his career, and virtually unchanged throughout his life, allowed the production of a prodigious number of paintings—most of them snapped up by visitors.

His first commission, in 1722, was from an Englishman. From then on Englishmen were his chief patrons. Joseph Smith, who was later to become consul in Venice, served as middleman, commissioning Canaletto on behalf of the Gentry, the Aristocracy, and ultimately the Royal Household itself. Smith's own collection of Canaletto's work, amounting to some fifty pictures, was eventually bought by George III and now graces a gallery at Windsor Castle.

In 1746, with the beginning of the war of the Austrian Succession, business became slack. Travellers from Britain thinned out. It was a matter of elementary logic that the painter, instead of waiting in Venice for the English, should come among them. By now not short of influential friends, he found his move to London easy: he brought letters of introduction. Tom Hill, former tutor to the Duke of Richmond, wrote to the duke saying that he thought that the best thing would be 'to let him draw a view of the river from yr dining-room, which would give him as much reputation as any of his Venetian prospects'. The duke agreed—and it did.

Canaletto settled in England and painted many scores of pictures, not only of London but of English castles, country

Canaletto, seen here at about the age of twenty-eight, was nearly fifty when he came to London. Beak Street was about the same age; it was part of the new westward wave of building that followed the Great Fire of 1666. (Regent Street, now close by, was then unbuilt; in its place was Swallow Street, a narrow thoroughfare 'long, ugly and irregular,' with a reputation 'by no means good'.)

houses, bridges, river landscapes, colleges and chapels. So full did his order book become, it is said that he continued painting English views—from memory and from sketches—after he had returned home.

The London of Canaletto's time was in some respects not markedly different from his Venice. The Thames was a major highway, with a multitude of craft of all descriptions. He painted, as he had done at home, the ferry boats, the processional barges, the skiffs and sailing boats of every day. He recorded the construction of the new Westminster Bridge, faithfully noting the planks, poles, scaffolding and mason's tackle. But it must be said that all his work had the same Canaletto look—the luminous, cloudless sky, the unending sunshine of the lagoon. He made London more Venetian than it was. He died rich.

Underground Station:
PICCADILLY CIRCUS

19

Marx analysed the British way of life with scientific detachment. He saw Dean Street merely as a vantage point from which to observe the bourgeois scene. He remained completely insulated from his social context. His poverty he viewed with a wry objectivity: 'My affairs have now reached the agreeable point at which I can no longer leave the house because my clothes are in pawn and can no longer eat meat because my credit is exhausted.'

KARL MARX (1818–83)

28 Dean Street W1

HERE, IN 1851, KARL HEINRICH MARX sat in a top-floor room writing the first pages of *Das Kapital*.

He had come to London as an expellee from Germany: Victorian England had provided him with squalor at Dean Street—and unlimited use of the British Museum Reading Room.

Apart from a revenue of £1 per week (received, improbably, from unsigned contributions as 'European Economics Correspondent' of the *New York Tribune*) Marx relied for the most part on spasmodic articles in newspapers and magazines. For the rest he was dependent on the charity of Engels, who was by this time working in the Manchester branch office of his father's textile business. Over the years the unfailing trickle of postal orders and cheques from Manchester kept Marx and his family alive. It was Engels who was to complete and publish the last two volumes of *Das Kapital* after Marx died.

The misery of Marx's time in Dean Street is almost beyond belief. His wife writes, 'At Easter our poor little Franziska fell ill with severe bronchitis . . . Her small lifeless body rested in our little back room whilst we all went together into the front room and when night came we made up beds on the floor. The three surviving children lay with us and we cried for the poor little angel who now rested so cold and lifeless in the next room . . . I went to a French fugitive who lives near us. He received me with friendliness and sympathy and gave me two pounds and with that money the coffin in which my child could rest peacefully was paid for. No cradle when it was born. Even the last little shell was denied it long enough.'

Underground Station:
LEICESTER SQUARE

20

A visitor to Dean Street reports: 'Disorder . . . manuscripts lie beside the children's toys, bits and pieces from his wife's work-basket, teacups with broken rims, dirty spoons, knives, forks, lamps, an inkwell, tumblers. But all this gives Marx not the slightest embarrassment . . .' Another visitor describes finding Marx busy at his desk over the latest chapter of 'Das Kapital' with one of his small children clamber-ing across his shoulders.

There were 40,000 ticket holders to the British Museum Reading Room in the late 1840s and 50s. 'Persons applying for the pur-poses of study or research are admitted every day, from nine o'clock in the morning till seven o'clock in the evening.' This was Marx's application for a ticket.

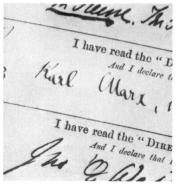

Hazlitt was born in Maidenhead, and spent his early days first in Ireland and later in America. But he was a Londoner, all the same. He greatly enjoyed walking in the town, particularly in the area where he spent his last years: 'Commend me to the streets and squares on each side of the top of Oxford Street, with Grosvenor and Portman Squares at one end and Cavendish and Hanover at the other, linked together by Bruton, South Audley, and a hundred other fine old streets.' The picture below shows Soho Square as it appeared at the time.

THOUGH HAPPY AND BRIGHT as a child, Hazlitt suddenly changed at adolescence. 'He passed under a cloud, which unfitted him for social intercourse,' wrote his father. He was to stay that way for the rest of his life. He worsened with the years. Coleridge described him as 'singularly repulsive—brow-hanging, shoe-contemplative, strange'. By the time he was forty-five he was an argumentative and friendless old man. A shambling, ill-dressed figure, he came to Frith Street to live out his last work.

Hazlitt—journalist, critic, essayist—had lived and written at a high rate of combustion. 'Whatever he did, creditable or discreditable, wise or foolish, he put it first on paper, and then upon the market.' But for all his brilliance and originality, for all his wealth of output, the market favoured him little during his life; money never came easily.

On one occasion, like Dr Johnson before him, he wrote to a London acquaintance: 'Dear Sir,—I have been arrested this morning, and am at a loss to know what to do. Would you give me a call to talk the matter over, and see if your influence could procure me any terms of accommodation? I am sorry to plague you about my troublesome affairs. Believe me, very truly your obliged friend and servant . . .'

First on to paper and then on to the market, from his rooms in Frith Street he now poured out the major work of his career, his monumental four-volume *Life of Napoleon*. He wrote, as always, like mad.

His facility in the actual business of setting words on paper was phenomenal. Visitors described how he would continue writing in their presence 'with wonderful ease and facility of pen, going on as if writing an ordinary letter. His usual manuscript was clear and unblotted, indicating great readiness and sureness in writing, as though requiring no erasures or interlining. He was fond of using large pages of rough paper with ruled lines, such as those of a bought-up blank account book—as they were.'

Hazlitt's admiration for Napoleon amounted almost to a fixation. A self-appointed minority of one in almost everything, it was typical of him that he should expend so much energy and

Starting life first as a theology student, and then as an artist, Hazlitt's first serious intention was to become a painter. He studied art in Paris for a while, but abandoned it for writing. His portrait of Charles Lamb (left) is in the National Portrait Gallery.

enthusiasm on so unpopular a subject. The book was not a success. Neither were his publishers. They went out of business still owing him the £500 he had been banking on.

Towards the end of 1830 he fell ill. His room in Frith Street became the subject of his last work, an essay in *New Monthly*, entitled 'The Sick Chamber'. On the afternoon of Saturday 18 September 1830, he died. His grandson, present at the time, recorded his last words: 'Well,' he said, 'I've had a happy life . . .' He is buried just up the road at St Anne's.

Underground Station:
TOTTENHAM COURT ROAD

Baird's career as inventor was beset by financial difficulty. It was while he was working on his own in Frith Street that Gordon Selfridge offered him the opportunity of demonstrating his (still unperfected) television principle at the Oxford Street store. The inventor was to appear personally three times a day and to answer customers' questions. In return he was to get £25 a week and all materials supplied free of charge. Desperate for money, Baird agreed, but the primitive image he was able to transmit at Selfridges proved a disappointment to the public, and the fatuity of their questions infuriated him. He gave it up.

STARTING IN BUSINESS on his own in an attic in Glasgow in 1919, Baird set up 'The Baird Undersock Co', a firm dedicated to the mass production of patent socks ('cool in summer—warm in winter'). Then he added another product, Osmo Boot Polish. Later he tried manufacturing jam, then selling honey, then fibre-dust fertiliser, then soap. Ill-health, bad management and bad luck brought each of these enterprises to nothing. He tried television.

The basic principles of television had been recognised for nearly half a century. No one, however, had yet been able to make it work. In 1922, ailing, inexpert, and almost penniless, Baird took up the challenge. Using the most primitive materials imaginable, and making quick sorties to the public library to inform himself on technicalities, Baird constructed a device. It was made of old biscuit tins, darning needles and a miscellany of electrical scrap. In the spring of 1924 he succeeded in transmitting an image of a Maltese cross from one side of the room to the other.

With a borrowed £200 he moved to London and set up his workshop at 22 Frith Street. Again, an attic; again, ill-health, poverty, and an almost pathological tenacity. On the afternoon of 2 October 1925 Baird rushed downstairs to the offices below and persuaded an office boy—one William Taynton—to come upstairs and sit in front of the device. Reluctantly the boy agreed, and became the first person ever to appear on television.

On 27 January 1926, still in abject poverty, Baird invited some forty distinguished members of the Royal Institution of Great Britain to witness a 'Demonstration of Television'. They crowded cautiously up the stairs to the top of the Soho house. In small batches, because there was not room for all of them at once, they saw television.

The breakthrough caused a sensation. But Baird's moment of glory was to come to nothing: while he had been working on his system, others had been following a different path. When the world's first regular service of public programmes was started by the BBC in 1936, the two systems were run for a trial period alternately. After a few weeks the Baird system was dropped.

'The Times' reported: 'The image as transmitted was faint and often blurred, but substantiated a claim that through the "Televisor", as Mr Baird has named his apparatus, it is possible to transmit and reproduce instantly the details of movement, and such things as the play of expression on the face. It has yet to be seen to what extent further developments will carry Mr Baird's system towards practical use. He has overcome apparent earlier failures . . . and . . . will be able to improve and elaborate his apparatus. Application has been made to the Postmaster General for an experimental broadcasting licence and trials with the system may shortly be made from a building in St Martin's Lane.'

brothers. and workshops of Mr. Marc...

THE " TELEVISOR."

SUCCESSFUL TEST OF NEW APPARATUS.

...embers of the Royal Institution and othe...
...ors to a laboratory in an upper room in...
...-street, Soho, on Tuesday saw a demon-...
...on of apparatus invented by Mr. J. L....
...who claims to have solved the problem...
...levision. They were shown a trans-...
...g machine, consisting of a large wooden...
...ng disc containing lenses, behind which...
revolving shutter and a light sensitive...
...was explained that by means of the...
and lens disc an image of articles or...
...standing in front of the machi...
to pass over the u... ...machi...
speed. T... ...

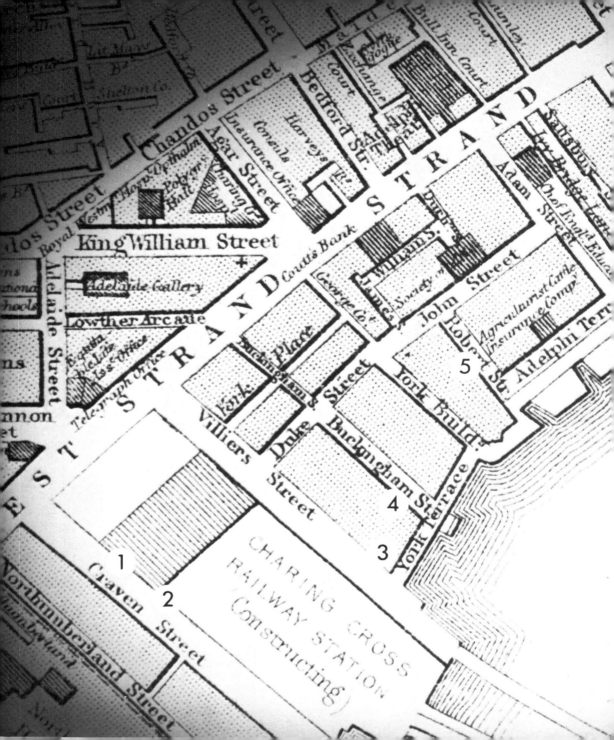

Chandos Street

Chandos Street

Bedford Str.

Bull Inn Court

Court

S T R A N D

Salisbury

Agar Street

Consols
Insurance Office

Harveys

Exchange

S T R A N D

Adam Street

of Bridge Education

Royal Lond Hosp Ophthalm

Polytec Charing Cr
Hall Hosp.

KING WILLIAM STREET

Coutts Bank

Williams S.

Duke

John Street

Adelaide Street

Adelaide Gallery

+

George Co.

Society of

Robert Str.

Agriculturist Cattle
Insurance Comp.

Lowther Arcade

James S.

Adelphi Terr

5

Bank
L.th Life
& Ins.Office

S T R A N D

York Place

Street

York Terrace

4

Telegraph Office

Buckingham S.

Duke

Buckingham S.

York Build

York St.

3

Villiers

Street

1

Craven Street

Northumberland Street

CHARING CROSS
RAILWAY STATION
(Constructing)

2

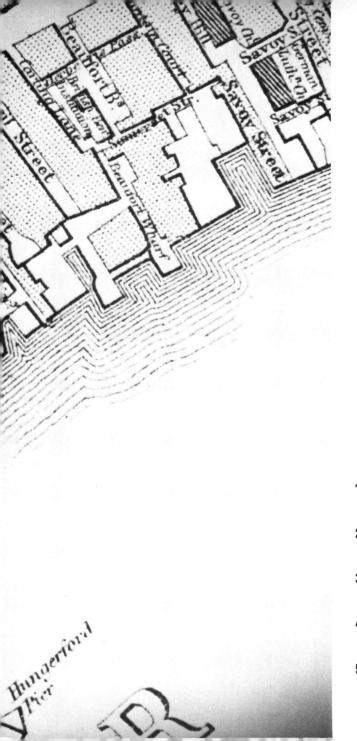

STRAND AREA

(Within 1 mile of Piccadilly Circus)

This map shows the Craven Street/ Adelphi area in 1863, some thirty years after Heine and twenty-five years before Kipling. Charing Cross Railway Station is under construction on the site of the old Hungerford Market (near where Dickens worked in a blacking factory), and Buckingham Street still leads directly down to the water's edge as it had done in Pepys' time. The Embankment was not to appear for another seven years. The Lowther Arcade, devoted largely to children's toy shops, linked Adelaide Street with the Strand. It was demolished in the early 1880s.

As a believer in the virtues of the minor comforts, Franklin was, perhaps, not quite a Londoner; he fitted one of the hearths in the Craven Street house with his special Pennsylvania Fireplace, 'a simple contrivance . . . for keeping rooms warmer in cold weather. Several of my acquaintances, having seen this simple machine in my room, have initiated it at their own house, and it seems likely to become pretty common.'

BENJAMIN FRANKLIN (1706–90)

'WALKING THROUGH THE STRAND and Fleet Street one morning at seven o'clock, I observed there was not one shop open, though it had been daylight and the sun up above three hours; the inhabitants of London choosing voluntarily to live much by candlelight, and sleep by sunshine, and yet complain, a little absurdly, of the duty on candles, and the high price of tallow.'

The logical and innovating mind of Benjamin Franklin was focused as readily on daylight-saving as on the repeal of the Stamp Act and the drafting of the United States Constitution.

He was almost a Londoner. He lived in Craven Street for many years and there were few points of metropolitan order that escaped him. At his door one day he found a woman sweeping the pavements with a birch broom. She looked 'very pale and feeble, as just come out of a sickness' and she told him that nobody paid her to do it: 'I am very poor and in distress and I sweeps before gentlefolk's doors and hopes they will give me something.' It was out of compassion for her that he paid her to sweep the whole street, but the episode aroused his interest in street-cleaning in general. To Dr Fothergill, 'a great promoter of useful projects', he proposed his plan for the more *Effectual Cleaning and Keeping Clean the Streets of London and Westminster.* He suggested that '. . . several watchmen be contracted with to have the dust swept away in dry seasons . . . each in the several streets and lanes of his round; that they be furnished with brooms and other proper instruments for these purposes to be kept at their respective stands, ready to furnish the poor people they may employ in the service.' As he rightly observed, the whole operation could be carried out, at least in the summer, before Londoners stirred from their beds.

'Human felicity', he wrote, 'is produced not so much by great pieces of good fortune that seldom happen, as by little advantages that occur every day . . .' He expressed the hope that his suggestion might be 'useful to a city I love, having lived many years in it very happily, and perhaps to some of our towns in America.'

It must be recorded that another point that caught Franklin's attention at Craven Street was Polly Stevenson, the landlady's daughter. They formed an attachment that lasted over thirty years, till his death in 1790.

Franklin first came to London as a journeyman printer in 1724. He distinguished himself on that occasion by swimming the Thames from Chelsea to Blackfriars, 'performing', as the record has it, 'sundry feats in the water as he went along'. He worked in the print shop of Mr Watts, near Drury Lane, and had lodgings close by. His rent was 1s 6d [7½p] per week. Thirty-six years later he returned, bringing with him his son William and a Negro slave. He settled in Craven Street and stayed for eighteen years.

Underground Station:
CHARING CROSS

Heine, poet, lyricist and visionary, was also a prolific writer on politics. He became increasingly concerned with the European political scene and with questions of social reform. By the time he visited London he was a keen observer of social conditions. The contrast between the classes in England 'smothers the imagination and tears the heart,' he wrote. He saw 'the lazy lord who, like a surfeited god, rides by on his high horse, casting now and then an aristocratically indifferent glance at the mob below, as though they were swarming ants, or rather a mass of baser beings, whose joys and sorrows have nothing in common with his feelings.' The contrast between the classes was to remain an inescapable feature of London for upwards of three-quarters of a century. Gustave Doré, who visited London in the 1870s, pictured these paupers sheltering under a Thames Bridge, not far from the spot where Heine stayed.

HEINRICH HEINE (1797–1856)

AMONG HIS MANY SUCCESSES Heine also counted a number of bad mistakes. One was his acceptance of his original first name: Harry. (This he was to rectify in later life when, as a 'baptized Jew', he took the name Heinrich.) Another was his acquiescence, at the insistence of his rich uncle Solomon, to going into business. To go into business at all was a false move; to go into business on his own was a disaster: the Hamburg firm of Harry Heine & Co, shaky from the start, went bankrupt within a year of its inception.

Another mistake on Heine's part was to visit London. 'Never send a poet to London,' he said. The weather was bad, he knew no one, he spoke no English and his health was poor. His highly successful *Reisebilder I* had just been followed by the equally successful *Reisebilder. II*. But his financial position was bad. Relations with uncle Solomon were strained and income from his work was unreliable.

On 23 April 1827, shortly after his arrival in London, he wrote from the house in Craven Street, 'It is snowing outside and there is no fire in my chimney . . . What is more, I am feeling ill and out of sorts . . . Living here is terribly dear so far I have spent over a guinea a day . . . It is so fearfully damp and uncomfortable here, and no one understands me—no one understands German.'

Although, when he got to look at it, London amazed him, it also appalled him. 'I have seen the most remarkable phenomenon . . . I have seen it and am still amazed. Send a philosopher to London but, on your life, not a poet! The mere seriousness of everything, the colossal uniformity, the machine-like movement, the shrillness, even of joy—this over-driven London oppresses fancy and rends the heart.'

He patronised the public gallery of the House of Commons, where he listened avidly to the speeches of George Canning, whom he much admired. He also patronised, it has been said, a number of the ladies of the town, one or two of whom he also greatly admired. He tried a trip to 'an English watering place'—Ramsgate—and shortly afterwards returned home in disgust. Vanquished by Britain's materialism, her climate and her cooking, he reached home a confirmed anglophobe.

'I expected great palaces and saw nothing but little houses . . .' Heine's image of London was one of endless uniformity. The 'little houses' (one of which was No 32 Craven Street) appalled him most. 'But the very monotony of them, and the infinite number of them, make a powerful impression.'

Underground Station: CHARING CROSS

In the 1970s the railway arches across the road still house a theatre. In Kipling's time this was the home of Gatti's Music Hall and Restaurant—an inspiration to him in its revelations of the realities of turn-of-the-century London. Villiers Street was 'primitive and passionate in its habits and population'; Gatti's he savoured for 'the smoke, the roar and the good-fellowship of relaxed humanity'. Beneath his window the ladies of the footlights would argue heatedly with the cab-drivers who ferried them from hall to hall.

Underground Station:
CHARING CROSS

RUDYARD KIPLING (1865–1936)

IN A SMALL SUITE OF ROOMS on the fifth floor of this building the Bard of Empire lived from 1889 to 1891. His reputation as a writer had taken time to reach London from his early years in India, but as he installed himself in Villiers Street he found himself newly famous.

He immediately set himself to fresh work here, but his readership was in the meantime content to be regaled with reissues of some of his backlog—work which had already appeared in India and elsewhere.

Though universally acclaimed, he was hard up. The rooms were 'small, not over-clean, or well-kept . . .' They were also conveniently close to the ground-floor establishment of Harris the Sausage King 'who for tuppence, gave as much sausage and mash as would carry one from breakfast to dinner—when one dined with nice people who did not eat sausage for a living. Another tuppence found me a filling supper.'

Though socially and geographically at the centre of things, his view of London was a lonely one. From his windows he looked out into the pea-soup fogs of the river. The Charing Cross trains rumbled across the bridge to the south, sometimes completely invisible. 'Once,' Kipling recalls, 'I faced the reflection of my own face in the jet-black mirror of the window panes for five days . . .'

There were clear days, however. From one of his windows Kipling could see straight through the entrance fanlight of Gatti's, the music hall under the railway arches across the road, 'almost to the stage'. The Victorian rumbustiousness of Gatti's appealed to him; its atmosphere is reflected in his *Barrack Room Ballads,* one of the works that the fifth-floor suite produced.

Here, too, he wrote *The Light that Failed.* In the story the building appears as a seven-storey structure, a gloomy monster of gas-lit London: 'The well of the staircase disappeared into darkness, pricked by tiny gas-jets, and there were sounds of men talking and doors slamming seven flights below . . .' In the 1970s the gas-jets have gone, a lift occupies the stairwell, and the building is called Kipling House.

London took Kipling to its heart when he arrived in the latter part of 1889. Nothing since Dickens had compared with his meteoric rise to fame. But the ensuing years were less ecstatic. 'The Light that Failed', written at Villiers Street, was to prove a disappointment.

The York Buildings Waterworks (above) was one of a number of installations designed to pump water from the Thames to various parts of London. Originally devised to work from the tides, some also used horsepower and later, in the early eighteenth century, some were converted to steam. The 'London Daily Post' complained that the 'York Buildings Dragon', as it was called, 'was attended with so much smoke that it not only must pollute the air thereabouts, but spoil the furniture.' To the right of the tower is the Watergate, in Pepys' time still in use as a river-barge landing place. Behind is the 'new' No 14, in which Pepys lived from 1688 until his retirement to a country house in Clapham in 1701. The 'new No 14' stood until 1791, when the present building was put up.

Underground Station:
CHARING CROSS

SAMUEL PEPYS (1633–1703)

Son of a Huntingdonshire tailor, Samuel Pepys was born in London and remained a Londoner all his life. He stayed at his post throughout the plague year 'as others of the King's servants faced the dangers of war'.

Buckingham Street, has been the home of a remarkable number of famous men. The present No 14 has housed Sir Humphry Davy, who is said to have carried out electrical experiments here, and William Etty the painter. Opposite, at No 15 (now demolished), Charles Dickens lived for a time in rooms on the top floor, and at various periods the building housed Peter the Great (1698), Henry Fielding (1753) and Jean-Jacques Rousseau (1765).

THE ARCH AT THE FOOT of Buckingham Street marks the northern bank of the Thames in former times. Known as the Watergate, it was a going concern when Pepys arrived at No 12 in 1679. So was the Waterworks, a less solid structure, which stood on the shore a little to the west, not far from Pepys' house, which was just two houses away from the river.

The Waterworks was a 60ft wooden tower, devised by its proprietors to carry Thames water first to a tank at the top and thence, by gravity, as far as Marylebone. In the early hours of 9 July 1684 the tower caught fire and threatened to burn down half Buckingham Street. As a preventive measure No 14, nearest to the tower, was blown up, lock, stock and barrel. Then No 13, next-door, was blown up.

Pepys, with recollections of the Great Fire still fresh in his mind, quitted No 12 and watched. Predictably, he lost a number of belongings in the confusion.

His years at No 12, though less spectacular than some of his Fire and Plague years, had been not without episode. He had come here at the invitation of his friend William Hewer, direct from a cell in the Tower of London where he had been held as a suspect in the 'Popish Plot' affair. He remained on bail in Buckingham Street until February of the following year, and spent much of his time and energy on the single job of clearing his name. The result—two huge volumes of documentation and sworn statements, which he eventually lodged with the rest of his books in the library at Magdalene College, Cambridge.

After the rebuilding of the houses next door, Pepys moved into the new No 14 (to be demolished and rebuilt in 1791). Now restored to his old post as Secretary to the Office of the Navy, he transferred all of the Admiralty books and papers to the new house.

The group of houses, known collectively as York Buildings, became closely identified with the Navy. Isaac Newton addressed a letter to Pepys in 1693: 'For the Honble Samuel Peypes Esqe at the Secretary of the Navy's Office, in York Buildings in the Strand in London.' Pepys did little to dispel the confusion. He once passed on to the Government a bill 'for carved work done for the Office of the Admiralty in Yorke Buildings'.

Strand
topic !

The shore of the Thames was, in earlier times, much nearer the riverside building line than it is today. This view of The Adelphi in the early 1770s shows arched vaults giving almost directly on to the water. The Embankment now runs along this shore area. Prior to the construction of The Adelphi, the building line at this point was even farther back. In order to carry out the work, the Adam brothers had to overcome fierce opposition from the Lord Mayor. As Conservator of the River, he claimed that the new buildings would encroach upon the waterway and deprive citizens of their lawful use of it. The site, which had existed as a water-logged no-man's-land for many years, proved, on the contrary, to be an encroachment of the river on the land. The Adam brothers won their case—but not before the passing of an Act of Parliament to regularise the position.

AS THE PLAQUE SAYS, Robert Adam, Thomas Hood, John Galsworthy, Sir James Barrie and other eminent persons lived here. Those for whom there is no room on the plaque include Joseph Pennell and Margaret Bondfield. Not only this house, but the whole neighbourhood abounds with distinguished associations. Garrick lived in Adelphi Terrace round the corner, Rowlandson died just up the road in John Adam Street, and Bernard Shaw lived opposite. (Barrie, if he wanted to show off Shaw to his guests, would throw cherry stones at his windows; his guests saw him 'and heard him too, when he came to the window'.)

But most fittingly remembered here is Robert Adam, whose name the street bears and who, with his brothers John, James and William conceived and built the whole of the area known as The Adelphi (*adelphi*: the Greek word for 'brothers').

Son of a Scottish architect, Robert Adam was the second of four brothers. As a family firm of architects they dominated much of the second half of the eighteenth century. In 1758 Robert established the family practice in London. By 1764 he could style himself 'Architect to the King'.

The Adam brothers brought about what they described as 'a kind of revolution in the whole system' of English architecture. The Adelphi, now largely demolished, embodied a new and refreshing concept in public and private building; from its beginnings here on a stretch of reclaimed foreshore, the 'Adam style' spread throughout the world.

Leased by the brothers for ninety-nine years from the Duke of St Albans, the original site was an evil-smelling mud-bank. But in 1771 a structure of brick vaulting rose from the shore. 'The change effected by the brothers was indeed extraordinary,' reports Peter Cunningham. 'Over these extensive vaultings [they] erected a series of well-built streets, a noble Terrace towards the river, and lofty rooms for the recently-established Society of Arts.' The finished buildings were a revelation.

But the project was financially perilous. Though David Garrick promptly moved into the centre house overlooking the river, the house-buying public at large was slow to follow. The Ordnance Department, which had been a likely tenant for the vaults, failed to appear, and before long the brothers were faced with bankruptcy. They took drastic action; they ran a lottery. Tickets were £50 each and there were over 100 big prizes. They sold 4,370 tickets and saved the day.

Of the original street names (John, Robert, James, William and Adam) Adam, John Adam and Robert remain. On the main site there now stands a block of offices called 'The Adelphi'.

SQUARE

SOUTH

STREET

FARM ST.

HILL STREET

SOUTH AUDLEY STR.

CHARLES STREET

CURZON STR.

BOLTON'S STR.

BOLTON'S STR.

BERKELEY SQUARE

BRUTON'S

BERKELEY STREET

BERKELEY STR.

P I C C A D I L L Y

PARK CORʳ

PARK LANE

CONSTITUTION HILL

G R E E N   P A R K

Buckingham Gate

Sutherland Hoʳ

St. James's Palace

Lit. JAMES

ST. JAMES'S STR.

KING STR.

JERMYN STR.

BURY

DUKE ST.

St. J.

BURLINGTON

BURLINGTON GARᵈⁿ

QUADRA

BR

PALACE

THE

GROSVENOR PLACE

CHESTER

UP BELGRA

WILTON STR.

GROSⱽ S.W.

ARABELLA Rᵈ

PALACE GARDENS

BUCKINGHAM PALACE

ROYAL MEWS

THE BIRD

Wellington Barracks

JAMES STR.

PALACE STR.

ST.

J.

ST.

P.

YORK

BUCKINGH

1

2

3

PICCADILLY AREA

(Within 1 mile of Piccadilly Circus)

This is the London of Disraeli and Gladstone. To the north, Regent Street and Piccadilly Circus have arrived; Shaftesbury Avenue is still to come. To the south, Victoria Street has appeared, linking Westminster Abbey with Victoria Station. In a few years the space opposite Buckingham Palace at the end of the Mall will be occupied by the Victoria Memorial.

BENJAMIN DISRAELI (1804–81)

Disraeli's eloquence availed him little at his maiden speech in 1837. There were catcalls, yawns and boos. As he finished he said, 'Though I sit down now, the time will come when you will hear me.' By 1852 he was Chancellor of the Exchequer. He first became Prime Minister in 1868.

The Prince Consort had been dead for twenty years when Disraeli lay on his deathbed in the house in Curzon Street. As a special mark of favour he was asked whether he would like the Queen to come to visit him. 'No, it is better not,' he said, 'she would only ask me to take a message to Albert.'

SAYS A CHARACTER in one of Disraeli's novels, 'I grew intoxicated with my own eloquence'. Disraeli knew what the man meant. So did Disraeli's contemporaries in the House of Commons.

This foreigner with an Englishman's accent, this 'meretricious oriental charlatan' as someone called him, was born at 22 Theobalds Road. He died at 19 Curzon Street. His life had been a tidal wave of words. Here, on his deathbed, as he corrected proofs of his last speech, he said, 'I will not go down to posterity talking bad grammar'.

He made no bones about his concern for his public image. Nor about the disadvantages of his background. He told his constituents, 'There is no doubt, gentlemen, that all men who offer themselves as candidates for public favour have motives of some sort. I candidly acknowledge that I have. And I will tell you what they are: I love fame; and it is a glorious thing for a man to do who has had my difficulties to contend against.'

He got all that he loved. When, at the end of a lifetime of glory and contention, he lay dying, the local authorities caused straw to be spread on the road outside the house, so that he would not be disturbed by the sound of passing carriages.

On 19 April 1881, a servant came out of the Curzon Street front door to hang a black-bordered notice on the railings, and the nation wept. All except perhaps, Gladstone, whose admiration for Disraeli was guarded. (It must be said that the two rhetoricians viewed each other with distinct coolness. 'It is a great relief,' said Disraeli, on an occasion when Gladstone's parliamentary career had suffered a temporary eclipse, 'a great relief that this drenching rhetoric has at length ceased.')

Disraeli got on well with women. As well, it would seem, with his wife (some twelve years his senior) as with Her Britannic Majesty, who did not conceal her regard for him. The Queen gave him a copy of her *Leaves from a Journal of Our Life in the Highlands*. He gave her one of his novels. He bought the Suez Canal for her and made her Empress of India. She made him Earl of Beaconsfield.

He wrote seven novels ('Ah, Madam,' he would say, 'we authors . . .'). The last of them, *Endymion*, paid for the nine-

year lease of the house at Curzon Street. 'It will see me out,' he said. It did.

On two occasions Her Majesty travelled in state to his house at Hughenden, near High Wycombe. On the first occasion she planted a tree in the grounds. The second journey was to lay a wreath on his grave.

Gladstone was not at the funeral. He had every intention of attending, but was kept away with a stomach upset.

NAPOLEON III (1808–71)   1c King Street SW1

AT SIX O'CLOCK IN THE MORNING of 26 May 1846, a workman walked out of the gates of the prison castle of Ham, near Amiens in France, carrying a plank on his shoulder. It was not long before he had discarded the plank and acquired a ticket on the train to Brussels. Louis Napoleon III, son of Louis Bonaparte, nephew of Napoleon himself, adventurer, visionary and opportunist, had escaped.

He crossed the channel that night and arrived in London as the Comte d'Arenenberg. He found London in a state of excitement. But not for him; it happened to be Derby Day.

After six years' imprisonment for the abortive affair at Boulogne where, with a handful of friends, a tricolour, and a few old military uniforms, he had attempted a triumphal progress, he was back in the 'waiting room' of Europe—the London that he knew from previous exiles.

Soon he was established at 1c King Street. As on earlier visits, he cultivated the right people, borrowed money, and bided his time.

Seizing his opportunity with the revolution of 1848, he appeared at the appropriate moment in Paris. His name rang a bell. In the confusion, he was an immediate success. Elected a member of the Republican Assembly, then President, the man from 1c King Street finally ascended the Imperial throne.

When he reappeared in London, this time on a state visit with his bride, the Press loved him. 'He was seen to point out to her with interest and pleasure the street in which he had spent those weary months of waiting, as amid the cheering of the crowds, the cortège drove slowly up St James's Street.'

But his career as Emperor finished at Sedan with a crushing defeat by the Prussian army. He wound up once again in England, this time at Chislehurst, where he joined his Empress in a last exile.

When he died, there was mourning not only at Chislehurst. Queen Victoria herself was 'quite upset'. She had, she records, 'a great regard for the Emperor, who was so amiable and kind, and had borne his terrible misfortunes with such meekness, dignity and patience . . . Such a faithful ally to England . . .'

Louis Napoleon was a Londoner of the very highest quality. 'There is nothing,' he said, 'comparable to the position of an English nobleman or squire.' On the very day after his escape from France, he was back with his friends among the London gentry. He dined with Lady Blessington at Gore House (above) in Knightsbridge. He was an old hand in London. He had been an honorary member of the Army and Navy Club, had frequented Crockford's, ridden in Hyde Park—a full-blown gentleman. Later, while waiting for the revolution, he was to volunteer as one of Britain's 150,000 special constables, sworn in to deal with the threatened Chartist rising.

This was the scene, in April 1855, at the Guildhall, when the erstwhile occupant of 1c King Street was received as Emperor of the French by the Lord Mayor and Corporation of London.

Louis made a better job of exile than he had ever made of anything. In his makeshift Imperial Headquarters at Camden Place, Chislehurst (above), he settled down to a benign ex-emperorhood. By now an impressive figure, portly, bearded and gracious, he acquired a following even among the British. 'He was,' says his biographer J M Thompson, 'always kindly, always friendly, and accessible. Occasionally he would take the train to London, stroll down Bond Street and spend an hour or two at the Army and Navy or Junior United Services Club.' He was the very model of a well-behaved exile.

43

The exterior of Schomberg House (of which No 82 forms a part) is unchanged since it was built by the Duke of Schomberg. John Astley, the painter, divided it into three parts, living in the centre section himself. In 1781, during Gainsborough's tenancy, the centre section was occupied by Dr Graham, the quack doctor. Among his exhibits was Emma, a near-naked 'Goddess of Health', later to become Lady Hamilton.

THOMAS GAINSBOROUGH (1727–88) 82 Pall Mall SW1

GAINSBOROUGH'S SOJOURN in Pall Mall (1774–88) was marred by only two factors: one was the presence next door of Richard Cosway, a foppish, intrusive and highly successful miniaturist; the other was Gainsborough's apparent inability to push his fees up into the Joshua Reynolds' class.

In spite of universal acclaim, in spite of his great success with royalty and the gentry, his charges remained much as they had been when he worked in Bath—thirty guineas for a head; sixty guineas for a half-length and a hundred guineas for a full-length. But the Cosway problem rankled even more.

Cosway was a little man, 'refined and vivacious of expression, full-dressed in his sword and bag; with a small three-cornered hat on the top of his powdered toupee, and a mulberry silk coat profusely embroidered with scarlet strawberries.' In the near-regal purlieus of Pall Mall Gainsborough found him a discordant and distressing note.

No less difficult was Mrs Cosway (who was also a painter) whose Sunday evening receptions were handsomely attended and whose guests' carriages, sedan chairs, link-boys and lackeys blocked not only Gainsborough's front door but virtually the whole of his street.

Gainsborough was keenly aware of appearances. He would leave his conveyance in a side street rather than be seen to arrive at his house in anything less than his own coach. (His own coach, it must be recorded, had had to be done away with; it was too expensive a luxury for his income at Pall Mall.)

He was also aware of his status. He was a founder member of the Royal Academy (Sir Joshua Reynolds was its president) but

Unlike his austere contemporary Reynolds, Gainsborough was an easy-going extrovert. As an amateur musician he embarrassed his musical friends, of whom he had many. Johann Christoph Bach found him one day playing a bassoon: 'Pud it away, man, pud it away! Do you want to berst yourself, like de frog in de fable?'

he had no compunction about quarrelling with it in public. In a final break in 1784 there was a row about the way a picture of his had been hung; when the Academy refused to budge, he withdrew all of his pictures and set up his own exhibition here in Pall Mall. He exhibited independently like this for the last four years of his life.

It was here that Gainsborough painted the 'Blue Boy', best-known of all his work, and here, in 1782, when relations were less strained, that he painted a portrait of Sir Joshua himself.

Van Dyck had been the inspiration of Gainsborough's early years. Tradition has it that in his last moments at Pall Mall he said to Reynolds 'We are all going to heaven, and Van Dyck is of our company.'

WILLIAM GLADSTONE (1809–98)
11 Carlton House Terrace SW1

Built on the site of the gardens of Carlton House, residence of the Prince Regent, Carlton House Terrace is rich in associations with royalty and elder statesmen. For Gladstone No 11 was a political headquarters as well as a home. From its staircase he often addressed meetings of the Liberal Party and here in 1873 he formally withdrew from leadership.

GLADSTONE WAS FOND of this neighbourhood; he lived, at various times, at No 4, No 13, and No 18, and for a little while close by at No 6 Carlton Gardens. (A few doors away, at No 18 Carlton Gardens, Napoleon III had stayed as guest of Lord Ripon in 1840 while preparing his descent on Boulogne. It was here that he and his friends occupied themselves designing military buttons for a 'regiment of the future'.) The Carlton House area was nothing if not select. It was also, as it is today, expensive.

No 11 Carlton House Terrace was Gladstone's home from 1849 to 1875. When he eventually gave it up it was because of the expense. It was all very well for the Cabinet to meet there occasionally, but one could not easily afford the luxury of such distinction. 'Nobody,' he told his wife, 'who earns anything under twenty thousand a year can afford the place.' They finally moved to Harley Street.

Dickens was a visitor at No 11. When he went as a distinguished guest to dine with Gladstone, he became aware that the dining-room was familiar to him. It turned out that thirty years earlier, when the house had been occupied by Lord Derby, a previous Prime Minister, Dickens had been called to the house as a junior reporter for the *Chronicle* to make a shorthand record of a speech that his lordship (then Mr Stanley) had delivered in the Commons. Dickens took the whole thing down a second time as it was declaimed to him across the room, this time with his lordship's afterthoughts and embellishments.

Of speeches and rumours of speeches, the house at Carlton House Terrace heard a great deal. Here Gladstone prepared many of the major performances of his parliamentary career. His oratory, whether at election time or within the House itself, was prodigious. Gladstone himself noticed it: 'Once more my voice held out in a wonderful manner,' he wrote after speaking for an hour and forty minutes to an audience of some 6,000 people in Liverpool. 'The hand of the Lord was strong upon me. Disraeli described him as a 'sophisticated rhetorician, inebriated with the exuberance of his own verbosity, and gifted with an egotistical imagination'.

The queen disliked him, too. But when he died he got a state funeral, and unlike Disraeli, an Abbey burial.

Gladstone was a prolific letter-writer—particularly to his wife, who often had to stay behind at Carlton House Terrace. When he was away, even for a short period, he would write at every opportunity, sometimes twice a day. For the most part his letters were background notes to affairs of state or blow-by-blow accounts of parliamentary debate; sometimes it was advance news of future legislation, or even budget details. Only occasionally did he allow himself tittle-tattle; from a royal evening at Balmoral he reported to his wife at No 11: 'The Prince of Wales had his usual pleasant manner . . . After dinner he invited me to play whist . . . The Prince has an immense whist memory and plays well accordingly. All the time there was the most execrable music I have ever heard: the Duke of Edinburgh on the violin, accompanying the pianoforte, out of time and most horribly out of tune. It was a truly astonishing performance.'

Underground Station:
T R A F A L G A R   S Q U A R E

ST MARYLEBONE AREA

(Within 2 miles of Piccadilly Circus)

1843: the London of Michael Faraday; at first glance, the London of today. The Botanic Gardens and the Toxopholite Society's ground are hall-marks of the period; so are the Diorama and the Coliseum, showplaces which lasted only briefly. The double line of trees across the park survives into the 1970s as a reminder of George IV's projected northward extension of Regent Street and Portland Place.

The next-door sycamore loomed large at war-time Hanover Terrace. Wells expressed his view of it in a special picture for 'The Countryman'. 'Like most of my erstwhile neighbours . . . next-door has gone away, but he retains his lease; his abandoned garden is a centre of weed distribution, and before I can get anything done about it, all sorts of authorities have to be consulted, and after that I doubt if it would be possible to find the labour necessary to terminate the ever-spreading aggression of this hoggish arborial monster . . . Every day when I go out to look at my garden I shake my fist at it and wish for the gift of the evil eye; every day it grows visibly larger, ignoring my hatred . . . This tree of mud, this dirty, ugly, witless, self protecting tree . . .'

Underground Station:
BAKER STREET

H G WELLS (1866–1946)

THE PREVIOUS TENANT had called it 12A, but Wells firmly restored it to 13. When the war came and the blitz broke all around him, he had the 13 painted even larger. The war drove most of the inhabitants of Hanover Terrace away, but he stayed put. More than once the front door was blown right in. With the cook and Margaret the maid, he stayed on, a defiant, tetchy, visionary old gentleman. He outlived the war by a year, almost to the day. He died in his four-poster bed in the following August, on the 13th.

This was the house with the garage at the back, whose walls he decorated with a cartoon frieze; the drawings traced Man's evolution from primeval slime to 1945. They finished with the words *Time to depart?*

This was the house whose solid walls were not proof against the blast of Wells' radio; as he grew deafer the radio grew louder; when neighbours finally complained, he wrote back saying that he would consider doing something about his radio if they would 'de-bark' their dog.

This was the house where the sycamore tree in the empty next-door garden brought Wells to the brink of apoplexy. It stole the life from his plants and blighted the whole of his garden. 'That bloody sycamore . . . is a complete repudiation of any belief in any intelligent god.'

Wells' latter years were shadowed by a sense of coming disaster. In 1932, in a lecture to students at the London School of Economics, he said, 'We seem to be living at present not in a civilisation that is fixed and working out its inevitable destiny, but in a civilisaton that is very rapidly going to pieces. The fate in front of masses of you may be much more vivid than the sort of fate that seemed to threaten us . . . The world is visibly collapsing as we talk here. There is something tumbling down, something breaking, something going out, and it is impossible to guess how far this ruin may extend.'

He died just after the exploding of the Hiroshima bomb. Over half a century before, in 1894, he had foreseen the possibility of unlimited power from atomic energy.

At 13 Hanover Terrace he wrote his last brief work: *Mind at the End of its Tether*.

Facing over Regent's Park, Hanover Terrace offered a good vantage point for Wells' fulminations at German air-raids. He continued to sleep upstairs throughout the war and was a rank-and-file member of his local Civil Defence unit.

During his last summer Wells spent much of his time in the garden at No 13. To his few remaining neighbours (most had left because of air-raids) his panama hat was a familiar feature. Lance Sieveking, who knew Wells, preserved the hat as a memento; it is photographed here on the lawn of Sieveking's garden.

The Post Office was proud of him: they said, 'In addition to his services in regulating foreign mails and country deliveries, he claims the credit for one very important improvement—the postal pillar-box.' Trollope's association with the Post Office lasted most of his life; starting as a junior clerk at St Martin's-le-Grand in 1834, he remained a Post Office employee—latterly a high official—until shortly before coming to Montagu Square.

Underground Station:
BAKER STREET

ANTHONY TROLLOPE (1815–82)

Throughout his years in Montagu Square Trollope maintained a strictly disciplined output. Not long before his death he wrote: 'It is still my custom, though of late I have become a little lenient to myself, to write with my watch before me, and to require from myself 250 words every quarter of an hour. I have found that the 250 words have been forthcoming as regularly as my watch went . . .' He calculated each of his books as so many days' work, checking them off as he wrote.

TROLLOPE CAME TO LIVE in Montagu Square in 1873. He had already published some forty novels; Montagu Square was to yield another nine or ten.

Trollope's exceptional productivity was the result of an obsessive self-discipline. Once having set himself to the idea of doubling up his clerkship at the General Post Office with a literary career, he filled every available extramural minute with pen to paper. Much of his work was written in railway carriages on official journeys; he devised a special writing pad for the purpose. It was in this form that most of *Barchester Towers* first appeared, with Mrs Trollope making fair copies of scribbled instalments as they arrived by post.

It was in the 'little backroom on the ground floor behind the dining room' at Montagu Square that he wrote the bulk of his work. It was here, too, that he completed the ill-considered volume from which his literary reputation has only recently recovered—his *Autobiography*.

Published at his request a year or so after his death, it revealed a conveyor-belt view of his work that shocked his readers. It portrayed the reading public merely as a market to be satisfied; it showed him as methodical, practical—and acutely aware of the economics of wordage. He kept account of his stock-in-trade, and of his takings, with the assiduous care of a shopkeeper. Production quota, delivery dates and word-counts were punctiliously adhered to.

The grand total of his income from the Montagu Square novels he noted at £15,600; 'I look upon the result,' he wrote, 'as comfortable, but not splendid.' *Barchester Towers* and *The Warden* had produced between them £727. His total life revenue from writing he placed at £66,939 17s 5d exactly. 'More than nine tenths of my work has been done during the last twenty years, and during twelve of those I have followed another profession.' He was in no doubt as to his commercial value in the world of books. Nor did he have much time for the distinguished personalities who put him into print. Of his correspondence with his publishers he said, 'I prefer Mr Longman's name at the bottom of a cheque.'

He died in a nursing home at 34 Welbeck Street.

Lear was keenly aware of his own oddities. It was partially to cloak his own embarrassment at the possibility of rejection that he devised many of his nonsense words. In a note to Lord Tennyson in the Isle of Wight he writes, 'Do you think there is a Pharmouse or a Nin somewhere near you, where there would be a big room looking to the north so that I could paint in it quietly and come and see you and Mrs Tennyson promiscuously?'

EDWARD LEAR (1812–88)

HE WAS BORN AT HOLLOWAY and died at San Remo. Between the two there was a wide variety of stops, most of them short. Ireland, Italy, Greece, Albania, Egypt, Malta, Switzerland, Rome, Hastings, Corfu, Jerusalem, Beirut, India, Ceylon . . . 30 Upper Seymour Street was one of them along the way. So, a year or so later, was No 13 Upper Seymour Street. So was Stratford Place, just off Oxford Street (where first the ceiling of the front room fell in and then the ceiling of the back room fell in . . .)

Lear, beset by epilepsy, by bronchitis, asthma, and personal unattractiveness, lived in the shadow of a deep disquiet. 'There was,' says his biographer, 'some hidden and unrecognised anxiety from which he could never escape, because it was part of himself.' It was almost certainly not just his asthma that took him so often out of England; it was a search for something.

He was a deeply sorrowful man. When Ann, his elder sister, died he wrote: 'I am all at sea and do not know my way an hour ahead. I shall be so terribly alone. Wandering about a little may do some good I suppose.' London offered him little in the way of comfort.

He was primarily a landscape artist. He gave lessons to Queen Victoria. But his humour, which served him as an escape-hatch from reality, eventually overtook him. The success of his nonsense was a joyful bonus to a gambit that began merely as a cover for his dissatisfaction with himself. 'How pleasant to know Mr Lear! Some think him ill-tempered and queer . . . his nose is remarkably big, his beard it resembles a wig . . .'— these lines from his self-portrait lend pathos to the image of the *Dong with the Luminous Nose*.

Successful as it was, his *Book of Nonsense* netted him just about £125 in all. He was unwise enough to sell it outright for cash down.

Nothing ever went entirely right for Mr Lear—in London or anywhere else. From lodgings in Corfu he writes: 'The people over me gave a ball; the people under me had twin babies: people on the left played on 4 violins: people on the right have coughs and compose sermons aloud.'

Lear took refuge in self-ridicule. He spent a great deal of time caricaturing himself, not only as in this sketch, but in letters to friends: 'Just now I looked out of the window at the time the 2nd were marching by—I having a full palette and brushes in my hand: whereat Col. Bruce saw me and saluted, and not liking to make a formillier nod in presence of the hole harmy, I put up my hand to salute—and thereby transferred all my colours into my hair and whiskers—which I must now wash in turpentine or shave off.'

Underground Station:
MARBLE ARCH

55

This was the shop in Blandford Street in the early 1800s. Faraday's employer was much struck by his apprentice's notebooks. '. . . these I occasionally shewed to my Friends and Customers. I happened One Evening to shew them to a Mr Dance Junr of Manchester Str who thought them very clever—and who in a Short time returned and requested to let him shew to his Father. I did so, and the next day Mr Dance very kindly gave him an Admission ticket to the Royal Institution, Albemarle Street. He attended and Afterwards Wrote out and Drew, making drawing of the Different Apparatus Used. This he took also to the Above Gent, who was well pleased . . .'

Underground Station:
BOND STREET

56

Of his reading in Blandford Street Faraday records, 'It was in these books, in the hours after work, that I found the beginning of my philosophy.' Twenty years later in Albemarle Street there is a diary entry after the series of experiments that were to lead to the production of the world's first dynamo: 'Experiments with a single wire. Beautiful.'

48 Blandford Street W1

MICHAEL FARADAY (1791–1867)

'THERE WERE PLENTY OF BOOKS THERE, and I read them.' It was here, when old Mr Riebau had the place as a bookshop, that Michael Faraday was apprenticed in 1804. He had served for a year as errand boy (it was handy to where the Faradays lived in Jacob's Well Mews) and at the age of thirteen he moved in permanently 'to learn the bookbinding and stationery'.

Faraday's father, a blacksmith who had migrated to London from Yorkshire, was glad to get the boy fixed up; there was no room for all of his four children in the cramped quarters over the mews coach-house.

Mr Riebau took a personal interest in young Faraday. He was impressed by the boy's capacity to acquire knowledge and he encouraged him to glean as much as he could from the books that passed through his hands. 'If I had any curious book from my customers to bind, with Plates, he would copy such as he thought Singular or Clever, which I advised him to Keep by Him.'

In 1809 there appeared a new edition of Dr Isaac Watts' *The Improvement of the Mind.* Faraday read it. Among its many items of advice it recommended attendance at lectures. Faraday attended lectures.

He compiled—and bound—notes on what he heard. These, together with Mr Riebau's kindly pushfulness, were to be the key to Faraday's whole life. They were seen by a customer who was a member of the Royal Institution, who showed them to its Director, Sir Humphry Davy.

So it happened that when Sir Humphry Davy wanted an assistant, he sent for young Faraday. He started him off at a guinea a week, with two rooms at the top in Albemarle Street 'with fuel and candles'.

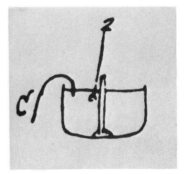

This diagram is Faraday's original sketch for the first electric motor. He drew it in the building in Albemarle Street (below) just about a mile from his starting point in Mr Riebau's bookshop.

Berlioz found his duties as judge of musical instruments at the 1851 Exhibition worrying. Unable to sleep one night, he made his way from Queen Anne Street to Hyde Park in the dawn. 'In a few hours' time I was due there for my duties as juryman . . . At seven in the morning the deserted interior of the palace of the exhibition was a sight of peculiar grandeur . . . A vast solitude . . . dry fountains, silent organs, motionless trees . . . I was just going to sit down in front of the Erard grand piano-forte . . . I was leaning on its rich covering and was going to sleep when Thalberg struck me on the shoulder and said "Come along, today we have to examine thirty-three musical boxes, twenty-four accordeons and thirteen double bassoons." '

Underground Station:
OXFORD CIRCUS

At the Manchester Square residence of the violinist Sainton, Berlioz met Wagner. Till then the two composers had viewed each other with reserve; afterwards, in a letter to Liszt, Wagner declared that he brought back from London 'one real gain, a cordial and profound friendship I conceived for Berlioz, which he reciprocates.'

58 Queen Anne Street W1

HECTOR BERLIOZ (1803–69)

IT WAS IN 1851, the year of the Great Exhibition, that Berlioz stayed at this house. He was no stranger to London; he had been here twice before. But this occasion was exceptional: to his surprise—and, it must be said, to his amusement—he had been nominated by the French authorities as a member of a panel of judges of musical instruments at the exhibition.

There was, he intimated to a relative, 'complete ignorance as to whether the English organisation has thought of reserving us a dog-kennel in the Crystal Palace or elsewhere, and so far our Minister [of Commerce] has not bothered his head about it.' In the event, Berlioz found lodgings here at the New Beethoven Rooms, Queen Anne Street—handy for the park, and unmistakably musical. 'The drawing-room, capable of holding at most two hundred and fifty people, is . . . frequently let for small concerts. There are many such given. My apartment being situated above the main staircase, I could easily hear the whole performance by simply opening my door.' He greatly enjoyed these gratuitous concerts: 'I opened the door wide. Come in, come in, welcome proud melody!' Less welcome was the warbling prima donna who sometimes followed. 'Shut the door, *shut the door!* Shut the second door, the third; is there a fourth? Ah, *the wretched* creature!' And then: 'At last I breathe again . . .'

His job on the judges' panel was not an unmixed pleasure. 'I have been in London for a month and a half, fully occupied with the stupid job of examining the musical instruments sent to the Exhibition. There are days when I am utterly discouraged and I am on the point of returning to Paris. You can have no idea of the abominable drudgery which is my special duty. I have to listen to wind, wood and brass instruments. My head splits as I listen to hundreds of the wretched things, one more false than the other . . .'

Like many others in the troubled years of the 1840s and 50s, Berlioz viewed London as a haven. In 1848, from London, he wrote: 'Flocks of frightened artists come hurrying from all points to seek refuge . . . Will the British capital be able to maintain so many exiles?'

Though he was insistent on the importance of cleanliness in the battle against bacteria, Lister himself often operated in his ordinary clothes, sometimes without even removing his coat. His 'antiseptic' was a fine cloud of carbolic acid, sprayed into the operating area by a pump (right). Taking off his top hat, Lister would roll up his sleeves, turn up his collar to keep the carbolic acid from his shirt, and begin. Anaesthetization was carried out by dripping chloroform on to a cloth near the patient's nose. Ligatures, at that time made of catgut or black silk, were often threaded, ready for use, in short lengths through a buttonhole of the surgeon's frock-coat. Apart from his instruments, all other equipment was drawn from the furnishings of everyday use.

JOSEPH LISTER (1827–1912)

WITH HIS UNORTHODOX VIEWS on operation procedure Lister was not popular among his confreres when he moved to London from Edinburgh in 1877. His choice of Park Crescent was influenced as much by his liking for the open country (Regent's Park is just across the road) as by a desire to remain outside the medical ambit of the Harley/Wimpole axis.

While most of Europe, and Britain at large, had by now espoused his concepts—first of antiseptic and then of aseptic operation techniques—London remained unconvinced. Surgery was still carried out by frock-coated men on kitchen and dining-room tables; masks, overalls and rubber gloves were unheard of. 'Hospital gangrene' was viewed as a normal hazard; the existence of airborne bacteria was discounted.

From this house in Park Crescent (now altered inside but externally unchanged) Lister conducted his campaign to establish asepsis as a standard operational practice. It was from here that on the afternoon of 1 October 1887 he drove with two colleagues to Somerset House to deliver the first lecture on bacteriology ever given in London.

The house had already acquired the research-laboratory atmosphere that was to pervade it for over twenty years. 'We found him in his shirt-sleeves . . . busy getting in order the exhibits for his lecture. Mrs Lister was also helping . . . There was a large number of glasses and tubes, culture tubes . . . some containing milk which had been acted on by various kinds of germs and some which had been kept successfully from infection.'

Lister's reception in London was discouraging; whereas attendance at his Edinburgh lectures had often exceeded 400, his London audiences were sometimes only a handful. Said a colleague, reporting on one occasion, 'Our hearts were chilled by the listless air of the twelve or twenty students who lounged into the lecture at Kings.'

But by the end of his stay in Park Crescent, in 1909, the position had noticeably changed. He had become Lord Lister, President of the Royal Society, benefactor of the human race. Unchanged in the simplicity and modesty of his manner, he remained 'at home' to students and doctors at No 12 throughout the period.

Lister, fifty when he arrived in London, had only recently developed his carbolic acid spray. This, centre-piece of his antiseptic technique, underwent many changes during his first years at Park Crescent. At one stage it was so big and clumsy that it was known as 'The Donkey Engine' and stuck out of the window of his brougham as he drove on his way to operations in the town.

Underground Station:
REGENT'S PARK

The picture below shows Shaw's view over the square. Returning one night from a performance by Vincenti, a ballet dancer famous for his leaping pirouettes, Shaw chose the roadway round the square as a practice track. '. . . I found Fitzroy Square . . . deserted . . . I could not resist trying to go round just once in Vincenti fashion. It proved frightfully difficult . . .' His account of the occasion records the intervention of a police constable, a police inspector, postman and a milkman—all of whom, Shaw alleges, joined him in the exercise.

BERNARD SHAW (1856–1950)

'FROM THE COFFERS OF HIS GENIUS he enriched the world.' Thus, the commemorative tablet. From this house he also enriched Fitzroy Square, not least with the verve and volume of his amateur musicianship.

His mother, with whom he lived here, was at times made frantic by the noise. 'I used to drive her nearly crazy by my favourite selections from Wagner's Ring, which to her was "all recitative", and horribly discordant at that. She never complained at the time, but confessed . . . that she had sometimes gone away to cry.' Shaw was not unaware of his limitations as a musician: 'When I look back on all the banging, roaring, and growling inflicted on nervous neighbours . . . I am consumed with useless remorse.'

He had come to live in Fitzroy Square in 1887. Starting as a clerk in a Dublin land agent's office at the age of fifteen, he had followed his mother's example and moved to London to make his name—and 'never again to do a full honest day's work'. She was a teacher of singing; he, he felt sure, was a writer. She supported him through his beginnings. He wrote a magazine article for fifteen shillings, a verse for a school prize book for five shillings and an advertisement for a patent medicine for £5. He also wrote five novels: all were rejected. By the time he got to Fitzroy Square, when he was thirty-one years of age, he had published virtually nothing.

In Fitzroy Square he wrote *Widowers' Houses* (1892), *The Philanderer* and *Mrs Warren's Profession* (1893), *Arms and the Man* and *Candida* (1894), *You Never Can Tell* (1895–6) and *The Devil's Disciple* (1896). Rejected, censored or dismissed as 'unactable', each of these was to wait upwards of ten years before getting a fair hearing.

It was while living in this house that his work as a music critic became famous. His pieces in *The Star* and *The World* had a big following. Later, as drama critic of *The Saturday Review*, he berated the theatre—the still Shawless theatre—of the day. He also found time for service on the St Pancras Vestry, where his chief concerns were improvements in drainage, refuse collection, paving, lighting, and the provision, for the first time in St Pancras history, of ladies' public lavatories.

Shaw, seen here at the age of thirty-eight, remained impoverished and unmarried until his early forties. Alice Lockett, a young nursing student with whom he was in love in his twenties, remonstrated with him over his financial dependence on his mother and the failure of his novels to find a publisher. 'Why don't you work?' she asked. 'I wonder how you will account for your life one day . . .' In 1898 he married Charlotte Payne-Thompson, who 'rescued' him from the squalor of his bachelor room at Number 29.

CHELSEA AREA

(Within 3 miles of Piccadilly Circus)

The Chelsea Embankment had been completed in 1873. The riverside homes of Whistler, Carlyle, Rossetti and George Eliot had become noisy with traffic. Old Mr Carlyle had died; then the others; the turn of the century brought Oscar Wilde, Mark Twain and Captain Scott—all within a few streets and a few years of each other. This 1915 map still shows the Apothecaries' Garden, but has already forgotten how to spell Carlyle.

JAMES WHISTLER (1834–1903)

WHISTLER STARTED LIFE IN MASSACHUSETTS and reached Cheyne Walk by way of St Petersburg, West Point, Washington and Paris. When he first appeared in London he lived at number 101, a few doors along. But after a brief return to Paris he settled in 1866 at 96 and remained there until his short-lived move to Tite Street in 1878.

Though much influenced by Japanese art, and though closely involved with Rossetti and his friends just up the road, Whistler was a lone figure in the art world of his day. His work was viewed in some quarters as a novelty, in others as an outrage. Of the four most significant pictures he painted here in Cheyne Walk, his famous 'Portrait of My Mother' was at first rejected by the Royal Academy and only admitted after special pressure from a single member.

His 'Nocturnes', some of them based on scenes of the river close by, were specially controversial. In these he made a point of rendering not what he saw but his remembered impressions. This apparently cavalier disregard for his subject matter infuriated his critics. When 'The Falling Rocket' was shown at the Grosvenor Gallery in 1877, Ruskin flayed it. Calling the artist a 'coxcomb', Ruskin accused Whistler of asking 200 guineas 'for throwing a pot of paint in the public's face.' The picture, which showed the artist's recollected image of a fireworks display as seen across the Thames, was certainly unusual for its time.

The episode proved crucial to both men. Whistler sued Ruskin for libel, claiming £1,000 damages. He won his case, but was awarded one farthing. The costs of the action, his loss of earnings while conducting it, and his backlog of extravagance brought Whistler to financial disaster. Ruskin, already afflicted by a brain malady and further burdened by the strain of the case, had been unfit to go into the witness box.

By the time of the action Whistler had left Cheyne Row to move into his new house in Tite Street. This, built for him by William Godwin, and a talking-point of the day, was the one that bore above its front door the legend *Except the Lord build the house, they labour in vain that build it. E W Godwin, FSA, built this one.* Within a few months Whistler was declared bankrupt and had to move out. The house, with all its effects, was sold up.

Whistler was a conscious eccentric. Joseph Pennell, who often visited him in Chelsea, says of Whistler in his biography: 'To be honest, my first impression was of a bar-keeper, strayed from a Philadelphia saloon into a Chelsea studio.' As he became more famous his oddity increased. His hat had a curlier brim, a lower tilt over his eyes; he invented amazing costumes . . . he was known to pay calls with a long bamboo stick in his hand and pink bows on his shoes.'

Underground Station:
SLOANE SQUARE

Whistler's studio was at the back on the second floor. It was to this room that Thomas Carlyle ('not a patient sitter') climbed the stairs for his portrait sittings; here the portrait of the artist's mother had been painted, and here, as Carlyle sat, the completed picture hung on a nail. (The picture is now in the Louvre; Carlyle's portrait is in the Glasgow Art Gallery.) To this back room also came the legendary Barthe, a French seller of tapestries to whom Whistler owed money. The Pennells relate the story in their 'Life of Whistler'. Barthe was told that Whistler was not in, but there was a cab waiting at the door and he could hear his debtor's voice. 'He pushed past the maid and, as he afterwards related, "Upstairs I find him, before a little picture, painting, and behind him the brothers Greave [neighbours] holding candles. And Whistler he say You the very man I want; hold a candle! And I hold a candle. And Whistler he paint. And he paint. And then he take the picture and he go downstairs and he get in the cab and he drive off. And we hold the candle, and I see him no more." '

Photographed in 1857 by Robert Tait, a friend of the family, this picture shows part of the 'soundproof' room built on the top storey at Cheyne Row. It was taken during the time that Carlyle was working on his 'Life of Frederick the Great'. In the three-tier bookcase, as well as a ninety-seven volume set of the works of Voltaire, there is a collection of books about Frederick; on the walls are maps, views and portraits relating to the period.

Carlyle made a point of studying portraits of his historical characters. 'Often I have found a portrait superior in real instruction to half a dozen written biographies, as biographies are written; or rather let me say I have found that the portrait was as a small lighted candle by which biographies could for the first time be read.' The pole propped in the corner was used to adjust the central skylight, the room's only light.

THOMAS CARLYLE (1795–1881)

24 Cheyne Row SW3

For this portrait of Carlyle his neighbour Whistler at first requested three sittings, but afterwards managed to get a great many. Carlyle disliked the whole operation and described the artist as 'the most absurd creature on the face of the earth'.

CARLYLE AND HIS WIFE LIVED HERE for nearly fifty years. When they moved in, in 1834, he described the place as 'on the whole a most massive, roomy, sufficient old house'. At that time there were only five houses in Cheyne Row, and this was No 5. The rent was £35 a year.

The Embankment had not yet been built (Carlyle thought it 'a real improvement' when it was opened to traffic in 1874) and the area combined an atmosphere of rural charm and river mystery. 'It was towards sunset,' Carlyle wrote in 1840, '. . . I went along Battersea Bridge and thence by a wondrous path across cornfields, mud ditches, river embankments . . . wondrous enough in the darkening dusk . . . and the very road was uncertain. Boat people sat drinking about the Red House; steamers snorting about the river, each with a lantern at its nose . . . Windmills stood silent . . .'

This was the house in which Carlyle wrote his history of the French Revolution (still unrivalled for its graphic narrative style) and to this front door came John Stuart Mill, pale-faced, to break to the author the news that the manuscript of the whole of the first volume of the work had been inadvertently used by a housemaid as a fire-lighter. When he had recovered from the shock Carlyle set to work to re-write it; he had kept no draft of the final text, and had destroyed his notes. 'Mill, poor fellow,' he said to his wife, 'is terribly cut up; we must endeavour to hide from him how serious this business is to us.' He re-wrote the complete volume in five months.

Carlyle's day-to-day life was bedevilled by insomnia, dyspep-

sia, and the noises of the neighbourhood. Despairing of sleep, he would leave his bedroom and stroll outside or sit in the garden watching the dawn; as for his indigestion—'I have a rat gnawing at the pit of my stomach,' he said, and was ill-tempered with his loving wife.

The noise problem, for a time, he endured. He put up with cocks crowing, next-door piano lessons and the noise of the Albert Bridge being built, till he could stand it no longer. Then he had a 'sound-proof' room constructed at the top of the house. It had double walls, a skylight instead of windows, and it promised complete insulation from the outside world. It was, however, too cold in winter, too hot in summer—and, Carlyle observed, 'by far the noisiest room in the house'. He came down to the lower levels again, finishing up in the dining-room on the ground floor.

Underground Station:
SLOANE SQUARE

ROBERT FALCON SCOTT (1868–1912)

Scott's biographer, Reginald Pound, describes him as a man who needed no uniform to give him his air of command. 'He was apt to be thought autocratic because of the cold reserve that he was capable of displaying in uncongenial company . . . His handshake was that of an entirely trustworthy man. He had a temperamental bias to the sombre side of things, as if at some formative stage he had learnt to be suspicious of life.' When Scott's sister was having her first child he was so overcome with anxiety that he fainted at the door of her house while waiting for the bell to be answered.

WHEN SCOTT GOT BACK TO BRITAIN from the Antarctic in 1904 he was made a Commander of the Victorian Order. He was also given the rank of captain and a pay rise to £410 a year. The money was not unwelcome. Although he had had little opportunity for extravagance on the Great Ice Barrier, family commitments were pressing.

He made up his mother's allowance to £200 a year and settled her and his two sisters here in Oakley Street. He also went to a first-class tailor and ordered a first-class suit. He wrote to their lordships of the Admiralty requesting six months' leave in which to write the story of the recent expedition. He was torn between the desire to tell people what had happened and the need for the observance of Service proprieties. 'I have no wish to advertise myself,' he said, 'I should be very sorry to do anything that the Admiralty thought unbecoming to a naval officer. Except in this matter . . . I am trying to keep as quiet as possible.'

Their lordships stretched a point. Scott spent much of his time at Oakley Street in writing and preparing lecture notes. Seven thousand people heard him at the Albert Hall; many hundreds of others heard him at other lectures up and down the country. His book, *The Voyage of the Discovery*, was the publishing event of the year.

Already the seeds of the next expedition were being sown. There was talk of new Antarctic operations by the Belgians, the French—and by Shackleton, Scott's sledge-companion of the Great Ice Barrier. There was also talk of getting married. There had been Pauline Chase (playing Peter Pan in Mr Barrie's new play), Mabel Beardsley (sister of the remarkable Aubrey) and Kathleen O'Reilly (friend of Isadora Duncan).

From Oakley Street Scott wooed Kathleen. She was staying close by at Cheyne Walk. 'Uncontrollable footsteps carried me along the Embankment to find no light—yet I knew you were there, and it was good to think of.' Miss O'Reilly became Mrs Robert Scott on 2 September 1908. In reporting the wedding ceremony, *The Times* appended a note: 'We are asked to state that the marriage will make no difference to Captain Scott's plan with regard to Antarctic exploration.'

With his colleagues Wilson and Bowers, Scott died in a tent in the Antarctic in March 1912.

Like most expeditions, Scott's relied for much of its equipment on the donations of manufacturers. One such contributor (below) was Dr Jaeger's Sanitary Woollen System Company Limited, 125 Regent Street, W. Another was the Civil Service Supply Association Limited of Chandos Street. Cadbury's Limited gave 3,500lb of cocoa and chocolate; Birds Custard gave 8cwt of custard powder and Coleman's gave 9 tons of flour and 'all the mustard the expedition would be likely to use'. Much of the planning for the expedition was done from Oakley Street.

tions. Style 366.

Price 2/9.
Sold elsewhere at 3/6.

JAEGER   SPENCE
           wear

Sizes—Sm

Colour Sh
Camelhair

" Shetland
(to slip
Camelhair
Natural
Camelhair
Knitted

THE 'SERVICE'   THE 'SI
                 WEAT

Underground Station:
SLOANE SQUARE

Born of Anglo-Italian parents in Charlotte Street (now Hallam Street), Rossetti was essentially a Londoner. Apart from a few brief visits to France and Belgium, his was the insular world of the ordinary nineteenth-century Englishman. He never set foot in Italy.

'Beata Beatrix' was one of the many paintings inspired by Rossetti's wife Lizzie. She was, said Walter Deverell, who first saw her selling millinery in a shop in Cranbourne Alley, 'a stunner'.

ROSSETTI CAME TO LIVE at Cheyne Walk after the death of his wife Elizabeth ('a noble, glorious creature' Ruskin called her) whose discovery as a shop-girl in a Leicester Square milliners' had transformed his life. Her death, from an overdose of laudanum, had shattered him; on an impulse of grief he had placed a notebook of his poems in her coffin.

Six years later, on another impulse, he applied to the Home Office for permission to open up the grave and retrieve the poems. He got it; three of his friends went to Highgate Cemetery and watched in the light of torches as workmen dug. Two days later the author was reading the poems after dinner to his brother William and Ford Madox Brown. They were published—the 'Lost Poems'—a few months later. In their first year they went to seven editions and netted him £800.

The house at Cheyne Walk was a showcase for his eccentricities. He filled it with antiquities—furniture, statuary, musical instruments and mirrors. He filled it with people too: the house served as meeting place, home, lodgings and *pied-à-terre* for a coterie of friends and admirers. Algernon Swinburne lived here, so did Michael Rossetti, his brother, and George Meredith. Frequent visitors were Burne-Jones, George Sala, Ruskin, Whistler, William Morris and Lewis Carroll.

He filled the garden too. At that time something over a quarter of an acre in extent, it became notorious as a minor menagerie. As well as peacocks (which his neighbours at first accepted as status-symbols) Rossetti collected an apparently endless miscellany of birds and beasts; ultimately the neighbours demurred. In its heyday the collection included a raven, a jackdaw, a talking parrot and a number of barn-owls; in addition there were rabbits, lizards, dormice, wombats, armadillos, wallabies, a marmot, a racoon, a deer, a laughing jackass and a kangaroo.

The poet's interest in animals was unaffectionate; he collected them merely as *objets bizarres*. The calls of the peacocks and laughing jackasses became the bane of the neighbourhood. The armadillos were a special nuisance, burrowing out of the Rossetti territory and, in one case, into the basement kitchen of a distracted neighbour.

It was in the room overlooking the garden that Rossetti produced many of his best-known poems and pictures. Here he

wrote *The House of Life* and painted 'Beata Beatrix', apotheosis of the millinery salesgirl. Other canvases were 'The Beloved' and 'Dante's Dream'.

The long five-windowed room on the first floor was the setting for the artist's frequent dinner parties. With its enormous hanging candelabrum, its long table and miscellaneous antiquities, it testified not only to its owner's taste but to his income. By 1867 his average revenue was some £3,750 per year.

For all his fame and affluence, he was unable to renew the lease at Cheyne Row without agreeing to a new clause—which became a standard item on his landlord's estate—that no peacocks be kept in tenants' gardens.

Underground Station:
SLOANE SQUARE

GEORGE ELIOT (Mary Ann Evans) (1819–80)   4 Cheyne Walk SW3

This was the house in the 1870s. Not far away lived neighbours Carlyle and Rossetti. George Eliot died in 1880, Carlyle in 1881 and Rossetti in 1882.

HER NOM-DE-PLUME was a refuge from Victorian mistrust of female authorship. Her house at Cheyne Walk was a refuge from the increasing hustle of Victorian London.

She had won fame with *Adam Bede*, *Mill on the Floss* and *Silas Marner*. Her *Middlemarch* was acclaimed as one of the greatest novels of the century. She was that unusual specimen of her times, a female intellectual. By the time she came to Cheyne Walk the secret of her identity no longer needed to be kept. She was a world figure in her own right.

Mary Ann Cross, who had been born Mary Ann Evans, and whose name will always be George Eliot, was charmed by Cheyne Walk. In the late 1870s it still retained the secluded atmosphere of what it very recently had been—a tree-lined rural waterside. You could still look across the Thames—'a very picturesque bit of the river'—to the trees, meadows and open countryside beyond. It was only recently that the Chelsea Embankment had come to breach the old-world privacy of the Cheyne Walk front doors.

After the death of Henry Lewes, the man with whom she had lived for so long, her health began to fail. It was in the last months of her life that she married the life-long friend of them both. She became Mrs J W Cross.

She wrote to a friend, 'Mr Cross has taken the lease of a house, No 4 Cheyne Walk, where we shall spend the winter and early spring, making Witley our summer home. I indulge the hope that you will some day look at the river from the windows of our Chelsea house, which is rather quaint and picturesque . . . Across the park and down Sloane Street would be a good way to us.' She was destined to live there for only a few weeks.

On the afternoon of 18 December 1880, Mr and Mrs Cross went to a concert at St James's Hall, Piccadilly. In the evening Mary Ann sat at the piano in the drawing-room of No 4 Cheyne Walk and played several of the pieces they had heard at the concert. On the following morning there was 'very slight trouble in the throat', but she got up for breakfast as usual and later in the afternoon she received friends to tea.

When they were gone she sat down to write a letter, but she never finished it. Three days later, George Eliot was dead.

George Eliot liked solitude. She had the advantage of living in a London where it was relatively easily found: 'I go out every day, drive beyond the ranks of hideous houses in the Kilburn outskirts, and get to lanes where I can walk, in perfect privacy, among the fields and budding hedgerows.' The picture (above) shows farm buildings near Kilburn Wells in the 1870s.

Mark Twain's humour concealed grief. The tragedies of his life (which included the death, while he was in England, of his daughter Susy) weighed heavily on him. In one of his later works—'What is Man?' (1906)— he turned almost entirely to matters of social philosophy. In a novel published after his death he reflects on the possibility that 'life is all a dream—a grotesque and foolish dream'.

MARK TWAIN (1835–1910)

23 Tedworth Square SW3

IN THE LATE 1860s Charles Dickens visited America and introduced the idea of 'the author's reading', a public platform entertainment for the masses. Standing in a blaze of light on a decorated platform, and reading directly from his published work, the author declaimed his lines as a dramatic presentation. The effect was often spell-binding.

At one such function in December 1867 the audience included Samuel Langhorne Clemens—Mark Twain—who on that very evening had just met the girl who was to become his wife. He was impressed by both encounters.

The public reading and the lecture tour became standard items in the literary scene. All over America, as well as in Europe, organised public appearances proliferated. Mark Twain, whose sense of public relations was never dim, joined in.

It was a lecture tour—a 'lecture raid' as he called it—that brought him, in 1896, to Tedworth Square. While here, he wrote some of his *Following the Equator*, a record of a world trip of which this visit formed a part.

Though threaded with the lightness of spirit that characterised all his public life, the tour was in fact in deadly earnest; it was an attempt to make good the massive debts he had incurred in imprudent business ventures. The Webster Company, his publishing house, had failed. So had the typesetting invention of James W Paige, another of Twain's enterprises. When he came to London he was bankrupt. By 1900, when he returned home in triumph, every debt was paid.

One unscheduled London lecture was delivered to members

of the House of Lords. It was on the subject of copyright, then under parliamentary scrutiny for possible legislation. Before a Select Committee of the House, Twain was asked his views on the duration of an author's copyright—what did Mr Twain consider as a fair and just time limit? Without hesitation Twain replied 'a million years'. He went on to give their lordships a colourful and extended address on the subject. 'I went on,' he reports, 'with the gentleness and modesty which were born in me.' Lord Thring, who was his chief interlocutor, was affronted—'plainly irritated', as Twain observed.

Mark Twain's view of the British, though still slightly incredulous, had modified over the years. On an earlier visit he had been to London with the express purpose of writing a satire, but the cordiality of his reception broke his nerve. He took refuge in writing *A Tramp Abroad*, an account of a walking tour in Europe.

OSCAR WILDE (1856–1900)

Wilde's first act on taking over editorship of 'Lady's World' was to change the title. 'The present name of the magazine has a certain taint of vulgarity about it, that will always militate against the success of the new issue. It is quite applicable to a magazine in its present state; it will not be applicable to a magazine that aims at being the organ of women of intellect, culture and position.' His appeal to the directors was successful; it appeared as 'Woman's World'.

OSCAR FINGALL O'FLAHERTIE WILLS WILDE moved in at Tite Street in 1884 when he got married. His wife was 'a beautiful girl called Constance Lloyd, a grave, slight, violet-eyed little Artemis' whose dowry paid for the lease of the house.

It was in the hallway of this house some ten years later that Wilde pointed to his accuser and said to a servant, 'This is the Marquess of Queensbury, the most infamous brute in London. You are never to allow him to enter my house again.' A short time later began the trials that were to end with Wilde's two years in Reading Gaol and finally his exile from England.

The house comprised the whole of the right-hand portion of what is now a suite of apartments known as 'Oscar House'. It was decorated, at his wife's expense, to Oscar's particular taste. The front room on the ground floor was his study; the walls were primrose and the woodwork was red. Compared with other rooms, its decor was restrained. In the 'first floor front' the walls were red and gold and there were divans and a glass bead curtain. The drawing-room ceiling, designed by Whistler, incorporated real peacock feathers. It turned out to be an expensive place to run.

As Wilde's son, Vyvyan Holland tells us, Oscar was then thirty years of age, married, his name known to everyone, with extravagant tastes, no money and no fixed occupation. 'He had achieved nothing so far but a reputation as a conversationalist and a great deal of notoriety. He began to look around to decide what to do next.'

After an unprofitable series of lectures (one of them, if the record is to be believed, at Wandsworth Town Hall) he settled down to a steady job as editor of Cassell's *Lady's World*. In this capacity he commuted for two years to Charing Cross on the tube from Sloane Square, walking down the Strand and Fleet Street, arriving regularly 'at a late hour' at his office off Ludgate Hill. But his enthusiasm for the job waned. He moved on to *The Picture of Dorian Gray* and *Lady Windermere's Fan* —and to Lord Alfred Douglas.

The house was almost ransacked by the predatory crowd that came to the auction sale as Wilde awaited trial in gaol. He never came back to it.

Underground Station:
S L O A N E S Q U A R E

During the first day of his brief freedom from trials, Wilde was hounded from one hiding place to another by partisans of the Marquess of Queensbury. He took refuge in hotels and boarding houses in various parts of the town, but everywhere he was recognised and asked to leave. He ended up after midnight at his mother's home not far from Tite Street. His brother Willie answered the door. White and dishevelled, Oscar tottered into the hallway. 'Give me shelter, Willie. Let me lie on the floor or I shall die in the streets.'

He died, in fact, in France in 1900. Half a century later, when the London County Council announced that a commemorative plaque was to go up on the house in Tite Street the decision was attacked in more than one quarter. One critic, a magistrate, described Wilde as 'a common dirty criminal'. The plaque describes him as 'wit and dramatist'

OUTER AREA

(Within 2–3 miles of Piccadilly Circus)

London, 1850. This was Dickens' London, with countryside just to the north of Camden Town, and the railways beginning to move in. Within a few decades there were ten main-line stations and the countryside had gone.

The period of Lawrence's stay in the ground floor flat at Byron Villas was overshadowed not only by the mounting intensity of the war but the affair of 'The Rainbow'. The novel appeared in 1915 and was the subject of a police prosecution. At Bow Street on 13 November it was described as 'a mass of obscenity of thought, idea and action throughout'. The whole edition was ordered to be destroyed. For Lawrence, this was 'the end of my writing for England'. He would go to America and try to change his public. In a letter to his literary agent he was defiant: 'I had heard yesterday about the magistrates and "The Rainbow". I am not very much moved,' he wrote. 'I am beyond that by now. I only curse them all, body and soul, root, branch and leaf, to eternal damnation.' But in another letter, written from Byron Villas on the same day, he confessed: 'I am so sick, in body and soul, that if I don't go away I shall die.'

D H LAWRENCE (1885–1930) 1 Byron Villas Vale of Health NW3

Lawrence was tubercular, and therefore exempt from military service. But his rejection of war, and the suspicions that stemmed from his having a German wife, made his presence in Britain untenable. The recruiting position, epitomised by the poster below, had become desperate. Many thousands of lives had been lost in futile fighting on the Western Front. Lawrence was disgusted, horrified and alienated; from Byron Villas he planned a new beginning elsewhere.

'YOU COME TO THE HAMPSTEAD TUBE STATION, walk up the hill and along past the pond to Jack Straw's Castle, drop down the Heath on the path opposite the inn, at the bottom swerve round to the left, right into the Vale, and there is Byron Villas before your eyes.' Lawrence's instructions to Lady Cynthia Asquith appear as a note of relief in an otherwise tortured letter from this address in October 1915.

The war had been on for over a year. Lawrence's resistance to the war, his discontent, his impatience with society's censure and his sense of civilisation's decay had embittered him. His instructions to Lady Cynthia continue without a breath: 'The only comfort in the long run is the truth, however bitter it be. As for the maimed and wounded and bereaved—even for them the only comfort is the utter truth—otherwise their souls are hollow.'

With his German-born wife he had watched a zeppelin as it floated in the night sky above the Heath. It symbolised everything that he feared—contention, the new technology and the end of old simplicities. 'We saw the zeppelin above us, just ahead, amid the gleaming of clouds . . . Quite small, among a fragile incandescence of clouds. And underneath it were splashes of fire as the shells from earth burst . . . It seemed as if the cosmic order were gone, as if there had come a new order . . . So it is the end—our world is gone, and we are like dust in the air.'

Lawrence and his wife were at Byron Villas for barely five months. 'We are struggling on with the furnishing . . . The infinite is now swallowed up in chairs and scrubbing brushes and wastepaper baskets, as far as I am concerned. I went to the Caledonian market . . . That is the reverse of infinity—a chaos, an unpleasant insanity. I bought one chair for 10/- [50p].' But by the year's end they were in a cottage in Padstow, Cornwall.

'The flat in the Vale of Health is empty,' he wrote, 'the furniture sold or given away, the lease transferred to another man. We go back there no more . . .' It was not long afterwards that he left England to spend the rest of his life abroad.

Writing, and roaming the world, he lived until 1930. He died in France. His ashes are buried in New Mexico.

In Keats' time Wentworth House was two houses, the division being to the left of the main door seen here, with an entrance to Keats' section at the side where the small annexe is now. Keats, in love with Fanny Brawne, the girl next door, sent her notes from his sickbed. '. . . You will have a pleasant walk today. I shall see you pass. I shall follow you with my eyes over the Heath. Will you come towards evening instead of before dinner? When you are gone 'tis past—if you do not come till evening I have something to look forward to all day. Come round to my window for a moment when you have read this . . .'

He did not marry Fanny Brawne, but she wore his engagement ring for the rest of her life. In Keats' grave in the Protestant Cemetery in Rome, one of her letters to him is buried—unopened. In his last days he could not bring himself to bear the sight of her writing.

Underground Station:
HAMPSTEAD

JOHN KEATS (1795–1821)

JOHN KEATS, GRADUATE of the Medical School of Guy's and St Thomas's Hospitals, Licentiate of the Society of Apothecaries, poet, lived here. It made a change from hospital wards.

Medical work had been gruelling; in his biography of Keats, Bates writes: 'He went his rounds with a tin plaster box containing bandages and implements for cleaning the wounds. He also handled routine cases in the outpatients department, pulling teeth . . . setting bones.'

The house, built in 1815, was originally designed as two separate dwellings. The single-storey annexe to the left of the building dates from 1839; it was added to make a drawing-room for a much larger house combining the two. When Keats came to live in the left-hand section with his friend Brown he was twenty-four. Fanny Brawne, youngest daughter of the family living next door, was eighteen.

It was in the bitter winter of 1819 that Keats came back one night from a trip to London. He came all the way on top of the coach. (It was cheaper in the outside seats.) When he arrived he was feverish. Brown persuaded him to go to bed. 'Before his head was on the pillow,' records Brown, 'he slightly coughed, and I heard him say, "That is blood from my mouth". I went towards him; he was examining a single drop upon the sheet. "Bring me a candle, Brown, and let me see the blood." After regarding it steadfastly, he looked up in my face . . . "I know the colour of that blood—it is arterial blood—I cannot be deceived in that colour—that drop of blood is my death warrant—I must die." '

In the candlelight of the room upstairs, Keats pronounced sentence. In Italy almost exactly a year later ('How long is this posthumous life of mine to last?') he died.

Someone said of him: 'John Keats was one of those sweet and glorious spirits who descend like the angel messengers of old, to discharge some divine command, not to dwell here. Pure, ethereal, glowing with the fervency of inward life, the bodily vehicle appears assumed but for the occasion, and as a mist, as a shadow, is ready to dissolve the instant that occasion is served.' As a poet, Keats' life-span lasted just about five years; for a significant part of it the bodily vehicle rested here in this Hampstead semi-detached.

Keats' medical lecture notebooks were embellished with inattention. 'The other day . . . during the lecture there came a sunbeam into the room, and with it a whole troup of creatures floating in the way; and I was off with them to Oberon and fairyland.'

Much of the last year of Freud's life was spent resting in the loggia outside the windows of his study at Maresfield Gardens. Though frequently in pain, for which he allowed himself only aspirins, he continued to see patients, relatives and friends. He also completed the manuscript of his last work, 'Moses and Monotheism'. The furnishings of his study, brought to London in their entirety, remained (and still remain) unchanged from their Vienna days.

Underground Station:
FINCHLEY ROAD

SIGMUND FREUD (1856–1939)

FREUD, WHO WAS BORN OF JEWISH PARENTS in Freiberg, in Moravia, lived in Vienna from the age of four until just after his eighty-second birthday. When, in 1938, the Nazis annexed Austria, his friends contrived to get him to London; Maresfield Gardens was his last address.

He reached England in June 1938 and stayed for a time at a house in Elsworthy Road, not for from here. ('I am almost tempted to cry out *Heil Hitler!*' he said, as he savoured the view of London from the heights of Primrose Hill.) Then he stayed for a few days at the Esplanade Hotel, Warrington Crescent, before entering a clinic for an operation—the last, as it was to prove, of a long series of such operations.

He came from the clinic to Maresfield Gardens on 27 September 1938. He died here a year later, almost to the day.

Ernest Jones, his disciple and biographer, records that he was delighted with the house, and said that it was too grand a place for someone who would not tenant it for long. The house became a focal point for the world of psychoanalysis and a place of pilgrimage for distinguished men from every field. H G Wells came here to meet him. So did Stephan Zweig, Chaim Weizmann, Professor Malinowski—and Salvador Dali, to make a sketch of him. (Freud's view of the Dali was mixed: 'It would be interesting to investigate analytically how he came to create that picture,' he afterwards wrote to Zweig.)

Freud's study and consulting room gave on to the garden at the back, and there was a canopied swing seat under the trees on the loggia outside the french windows. This area of quiet and relaxation was at the centre of Freud's life throughout his last months.

He was fully resigned to his condition: 'There is no longer any doubt,' he wrote in March 1939, 'that I have a new recurrence of my dear old cancer, with which I have been sharing my existence for sixteen years . . .' He was resting on the garden seat on the morning of 3 September 1939 when he heard the first air-raid warning of World War II. He betrayed no concern. When a radio broadcast spoke of the war as being probably the last, his only comment was, 'It is most definitely *my* last war.'

Freud stood his ground when the Nazis invaded Austria in 1938. Only reluctantly did he accept efforts on his behalf to get him to London. This picture, hitherto unpublished, and among the last to be taken of him, shows him about to enter the Paddington hotel in which he stayed briefly after his arrival in Britain in June 1938. From here, after a final operation at a London clinic, he moved to the house at Maresfield Gardens.

'An invention for improvements in transmitting electrical impulses and signals and in apparatus therefor . . .' This, the world's first patent for a system of wireless telegraphy, was granted on 2 June 1896 to *'Guglielmo Marconi of 71 Hereford Road, Bayswater in the County of Middlesex'*. The application had declared that *'according to this invention electrical actions or manifestations are transmitted through the air, earth or water, by means of electric oscillations of high frequency . . .'* In just over a year, with transmissions extending to 18 miles, the *'Wireless Telegraph & Signal Company'* was formed.

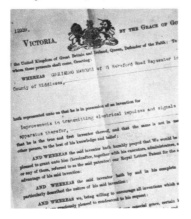

Underground Station:
BAYSWATER

GUGLIELMO MARCONI (1874–1937)

Not least of Marconi's difficulties was his extreme youth; his elders, both in Italy and in Britain, were sceptical. His appearance in photographs tended to accentuate his 'schoolboy look'. This picture was taken shortly after his application to the British Post Office for permission to demonstrate his invention.

The visiting card of Guglielmo Marconi—of Bologna and Bayswater. Passed on by his sponsor, Campbell-Swinton, to William Preece of the General Post Office, the card shows signs of excitement: someone—Marconi himself?—has made an error in the house number.

TO THIS 'SUBSTANTIAL AND DECOROUS' HOUSE, in 1896, came Signora Marconi with her twenty-two-year-old son Guglielmo. The Italian Government had been unenthusiastic about Guglielmo's proposals for 'wire-less telegraphy', and friends of the Irish-Italian Marconi family had suggested London.

The young Marconi had already carried out successful transmissions in the grounds of the family villa at Pontecchio. Now, in two top-floor rooms at the front of the house in Hereford Road, he gathered equipment together to repeat his experiments for the British.

It was from here that he sought the aid of British patent agents, from here that he approached the technical experts of the General Post Office. Here his mother sat with him 'in a large room with wires all round' taking careful records of his experiments, and transcribing them in copper-plate script.

To the house came cousin Henry (Henry Jameson-Davis, who had helped with advice and introductions when the Marconis first arrived) and technicians and physicists of his acquaintance. They were impressed by what they saw. It was clear that here was not just a new device—a new age was being born. 'The clicking transmitter on the table in Bayswater was signalling the end of a way of life . . .'

Writing to Sir William Preece of the General Post Office, Mr Campbell-Swinton, the leading electrical engineer of the day, introduced Marconi: 'He appears to have got considerably beyond what I believe other people have done in this line.' Within only a few weeks of his arrival in England, Marconi was invited to the Post Office headquarters in St Martin's-le-Grand. In a crucial trial from the roof of the building, transmission was attempted from the GPO to a point half a mile away. When the moment came, the twenty-two-year-old Italian tapped out a message on the transmitter; within seconds the text was being returned by the distant operator. The GPO was impressed.

In the upstairs room at Hereford Road, only four months after being met by cousin Henry at Victoria Station, the Marconis completed an application for a patent—the world's first application for a patent for wireless telegraphy. Signora Marconi wrote it out neatly in copper-plate script.

THIS PLAQUE COMMEMORATES THE
DISCOVERY IN THIS ROOM OF
PENICILLIN
BY SIR ALEXANDER FLEMING
IN SEPTEMBER 1928
TO THE GLORY OF GOD
AND IMMEASURABLE BENEFIT TO
MANKIND

Fleming did not actually live in his St Mary's laboratory (now marked with a plaque) but he came very close to doing so. He came to Praed Street in 1901 and remained there until 1954. He often worked until very late at night. Students returning from parties relied on finding him still at his microscope at two in the morning. During World War II, after being bombed out of his house in Chelsea, he spent almost every night at the hospital, sleeping in a basement dormitory. He occupied the small laboratory (the interior appears below) from 1920 until the early 1930s.

PRAED
STREET

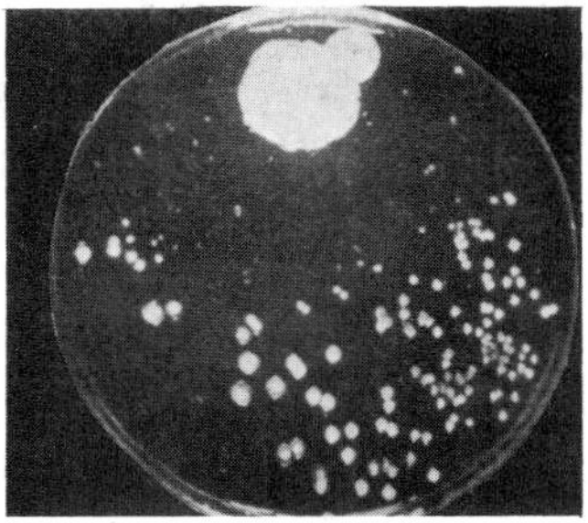

This is the original 'Praed Street dish'. It contains, toward the top of the picture, fully formed colonies of staphylococcus, and in the lower part, the mould that developed from the spore that fell by chance on the dish. The blank area around the intruder indicates the destruction of staphylococcus microbes. Fleming said, 'It arrived nameless and numberless—all I did was to notice it.'

St Mary's Hospital Praed Street W2 **ALEXANDER FLEMING** (1881–1955)

IF FLEMING HAD NOT ALSO BEEN A GENIUS his success might almost have been viewed as a matter of pure chance. He went into medicine largely because his brother had done so. He had gone to St Mary's hospital because, as a student, he had played their team at water polo. He became a bacteriologist because he was a good marksman: the Bacteriology Department wanted him for their rifle club. When he discovered the properties of penicillin it was as a result of the chance arrival through his Praed Street window of a certain particle of mould spore.

In September 1928, Fleming took up a culture dish which had been among others near the open laboratory window, and as a matter of routine, inspected it. It had contained a culture of staphylococcus, the micro-organism that causes boils and other infections. But now, as he narrowly observed, the growth of the culture had been disturbed. A mould had appeared in the dish—something brought in from outside on a draught of air. In the immediate area of the intrusive mould the dish was clear; the mould had dissolved the colonies of staphylococcus surrounding it. This incident, 'a triumph of accident and shrewd observation', was the start of a process that was to lead, in the late 1940s, to the mass production of the most powerful antibiotic the world has known.

Fleming, a reserved, chain-smoking Scot, spent most of his last years in the study of moulds. On one occasion, speaking to a group of artists, he said, 'If any of you gentlemen has a pair of mouldy old shoes, I'd very much like to have them.'

He became a Fellow of the Royal Society in 1943, was knighted in 1944 and received a Nobel Laureate in 1945.

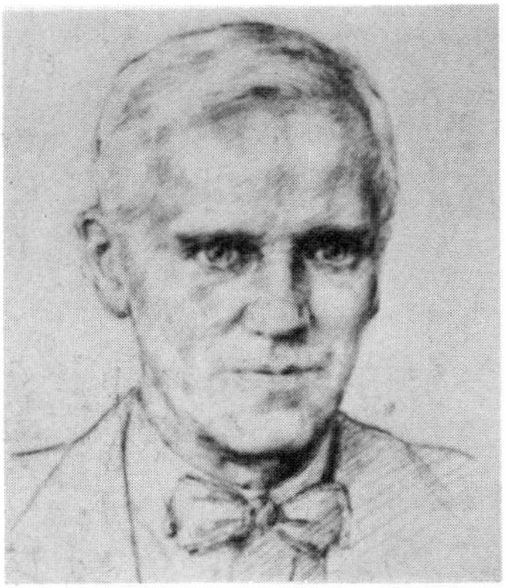

'As soon as you uncover a culture dish', said Fleming, 'something tiresome is sure to happen. Things fall out of the air.' To the Praed Street specimen, which he identified as penicillium notatum, he gave the name 'penicillin'.

Underground Station:
PADDINGTON

The house was the first formal United States Embassy in London. Prior to its adoption by the US Government, ambassadorial accommodation and living expenses were defrayed by ambassadors themselves from their private resources. It was Walter Page, appointee of Woodrow Wilson, who urged that America's London ambassador be given his due status. He wrote home: 'It is regarded as a poor compliment that our Government has no home here and skimps our ambassador . . .' His insistence had its outcome in J Pierpont Morgan's gift of 14 Prince's Gate.

JOHN F KENNEDY (1917–63)

ORIGINALLY TWO HOUSES (No 13 was suppressed by annexation some time in the 1870s), the building was the property of the Morgan family. It was occupied first by Junius Spencer, then by John Pierpont, then by John Pierpont Jr. It served the second and third generation not only as a town house but as a museum-cum-gallery for a massive art collection. Both men were rich; both were connoisseurs. In the early 1920s J Pierpont Morgan Jr presented the building to the US Government.

In the 1920s and 1930s it served as the American Embassy in London. To it, as Ambassador, came Joseph P Kennedy in 1938 with his wife and nine children.

Life magazine commented, 'Whether or not Franklin Roosevelt thought of it beforehand, it has turned out that when he appointed Mr Kennedy to be Ambassador to Great Britain he got eleven ambassadors for the price of one.' At first there were Teddy, Jean, Bobby, Patricia, Rosemary, Kathleen and Eunice. Later came Joe and the other son John Fitzgerald Kennedy.

John F Kennedy, barely out of his teens, had spent four years at high school and a few months at Princeton. Now he signed on at the London School of Economics. At the LSE—'a mecca' as one biographer describes it, 'for domestic socialists and revolutionaries from all parts of the Empire'—he was placed under the care and tutelage of Harold Laski, an old friend of Franklin Roosevelt. 'My father wanted me to see both sides of the street,' said young Kennedy.

Unlike their ambassadorial predecessors, the Kennedy family took a relaxed view of their surroundings at Prince's Gate. In the palatial, thirty-six room embassy, at his first press conference, Joseph Kennedy spoke to British press reporters with his feet on the desk. His son John, whatever else he may have achieved at the London School of Economics, soon acquired a reputation for originality in English spelling—never his strongest subject. It was at about this period that his family received a note from him saying that he had 'learnt to play baggamon'.

London's impact on Kennedy was short-lived. Ill-health, which had dogged him since his earliest years, intervened—this time in the form of jaundice. Kennedy's impact on the LSE was also marginal; it is said that on his election as President of the United States in 1960, one LSE publication carried a brief news item under the heading 'Old Student's Success'.

PARK CRESCENT

London's monument to John Kennedy is at International Students House, Park Crescent. The bust is the work of the American sculptor Jacques Lipchitz and is a facsimile of works by the same artist at Harvard and the Library of Congress. It was erected following a national appeal sponsored by the London 'Daily Telegraph'. The picture shows Robert and Edward Kennedy taking part in the unveiling ceremony in May 1965.

Underground Station:
KNIGHTSBRIDGE

In his efforts to bring his son to the fore, Leopold Mozart was often over-zealous. The language and manner of this announcement in the London 'Public Advertiser' was typical of his approach. A series of such notices appeared in the London press throughout their stay. Advertisements in similar vein were also published in Holland during the next stage of the tour, but thereafter, as the group neared Vienna, the idea was quietly dropped.

To all Lovers of Sciences.

THE greatest Prodigy that Europe, or that even Human Nature has to boast of, is, without Contradiction, the little German Boy WOLFGANG MOZART; a Boy, Eight Years old, who has, and indeed very justly, raised the Admiration not only of the greatest Men, but also of the greatest Musicians in Europe. It is hard to say, whether his Execution upon the Harpsichord and his playing and singing at Sight, or his own Caprice, Fancy, and Compositions for all Instruments, are most astonishing. The Father of this Miracle, being obliged by Desire of several Ladies and Gentlemen to postpone, for a very short Time, his Departure from England, will give an Opportunity to hear this little Composer and his Sister, whose musical Knowledge wants not Apology. Performs every Day in the Week, from Twelve to Three o'Clock in the Great Room, at the Swan and Hoop, Cornhill. Admittance 2s. 6d. each Person.

The two Children will play also together with four Hands upon the same Harpsichord, and put upon it a Handkerchief, without seeing the Keys.

WOLFGANG MOZART (1756–91)

IN 1764, WHEN LEOPOLD MOZART brought his children to London in the course of a European tour, Ebury Street was called Five Fields Row. This house, now 180 Ebury Street, was the home of the Randall family; for a few weeks, while Leopold was recovering from a throat infection, it was also the home of the three Mozarts.

Nännerl, the daughter, was aged thirteen; Wolferl (Wolfgang Amadeus Mozart) was aged eight. The children were prodigies, as Leopold's press advertisements made clear. Both were presented almost in the manner of circus acts. Accompanied by his sister ('whose musical knowledge wants not Apology') the young Mozart performed in public 'every day from Twelve to Three' in the Great Room at the *Swan and Hoop* tavern, Cornhill.

Fresh from successes on the Continent, where he had charmed everyone—crowned heads and all, the trio had found in London a slightly less ecstatic reception. They were received at court, and three times gave concerts to their majesties (honorarium, 24 guineas a time), but there was a distinct recession of interest. While father Leopold recovered, the boy took the opportunity of composing a few short pieces for dedication to Queen Charlotte. These, six sonatas for the harpsichord, were afterwards to be had of Mr Williamson in Frith Street (then Thrift Street), Soho. It was at Mr Williamson's, corsetmaker of that address, that the Mozarts finally settled when father's health improved.

Though less salubrious than the open air of Five Fields Row, Thrift Street was a cut above the Mozarts' earlier pied-à-terre off St Martin's Lane. There, with similar arrangements as to sheet music and concert tickets, they had lodged with one John Cousins, hair-cutter, of Cecil Court.

The Mozarts' stay in London—six months in all—was not as rewarding as Leopold had hoped. Wolfgang had undoubtedly made his mark, but there had been too much pressure, too much forcing of the pace. By the time the trio reached home again in Vienna, exhausted, ailing and slightly querulous, the child prodigies had become noticeably more grown-up—no longer fitting subjects for advertisements in newspapers.

Wolfgang Mozart played minuets when he was four and composed music at the age of five. His musical precocity was so extraordinary that Daines Barrington, the lawyer and naturalist, carried out a special study of the boy: 'I was witness of his most extraordinary abilities as a musician . . . I must own that I could not help suspecting that his father had imposed as to the age of the boy, though . . . he had all the actions of that stage of life. For example, while he was playing . . . a favourite cat came in, upon which he . . . left his harpsichord, nor could we bring him back for a considerable time.'

Underground Station:
VICTORIA

95

Though still new to his reputation as a writer, Dickens was already firmly set on the course of social reform. It was from Doughty Street that he wrote to the man in charge of the press reporters in the City Courts: 'In my next number of "Oliver Twist" I must have a magistrate; and casting about for a magistrate whose harshness and insolence would render him a fit subject to be "shewn up", I have stumbled upon Mr Laing of Hatton Garden celebrity. I know the man's character perfectly well. But as it would be necessary to describe his appearance also, I ought to have seen him, which (fortunately or unfortunately as the case may be) I have never done . . . It occurred to me that perhaps I might under your auspices be smuggled into the Hatton Office for a few moments some morning . . .' Mr Laing appeared in the July instalment of 'Oliver Twist' as Mr Fang.

Underground Station:
CHANCERY LANE

Maclise's drawing of Dickens with his wife and Mary Hogarth epitomises the spirit of the ménage at the house in Doughty Street.

Of his many London addresses, Doughty Street held the most poignant memories. It was in this house that Dickens made his only attempt at keeping a diary. It was intended to receive 'what rises to my lips—my mental lips at least—without reserve'. It covers just fifteen days, finishing on Monday 15 January 1838: 'Here ends this brief attempt . . . I grow sad over this checking off of the days, and can't do it.' Among its few entries there are frequent nostalgic references to Mary Hogarth.

WHEN DICKENS CAME TO LIVE HERE in the spring of 1837 (£80 a year for a three-year lease) Doughty Street was a 'genteel private street with a lodge at each end and gates that were closed at night by a porter in a gold-laced hat and a mulberry-coloured coat with the Doughty arms on its buttons.'

It was here, in a period of spectacular ascendancy, that he wrote the last of the monthly instalments of *Pickwick Papers*. It was here that he wrote *Oliver Twist*, from here that he journeyed to the schools of Yorkshire for *Nicholas Nickleby*; here he started *Barnaby Rudge*. It was this house that was to serve as a stepping stone from the obscurity of Furnival's Inn to the 'undeniable situation and excessive splendour' of No 1 Devonshire Terrace, Regent's Park. It was also the house in which his wife's sister, Mary Hogarth, died.

The tragedy of Mary Hogarth's death hangs, heavy with significance, not only over Doughty Street, but over Dickens' whole life.

'From the day of our marriage the dear girl had been the grace and life of our home . . . I have lost the dearest friend I ever had. Words cannot describe the pride I felt in her, and the devoted attachment I bore her . . . She had not a single fault . . .'

He mourned her with a fearful—almost a pathological—intensity. He even planned that on his death he would be buried with her. When it became apparent that others in her family had stronger claims to this privilege he was disconsolate: 'It is a great trial to me to give up Mary's grave; greater than I can possibly express.' Five years later he was writing to his friend Forster, 'I cannot bear the thought of being excluded from her dust. It is like losing her a second time.'

She appears, in various guises, throughout his work. She is Florence in *Dombey and Son*, Agnes in *David Copperfield*, and she is Little Dorrit. She died in her little room at the back on the second floor at No 48. She was seventeen.

To his wife, Dickens remained for many years 'ever, my dear Kate, your affectionate husband', but the memory of her sister never left him.

The Dictionary, prepared in its entirety at this address, was published in two volumes at £4 10s (£4.50) the set. Most of its 41,000 entries display an appropriate sense of academic detachment, but there are strongly personal touches. Querulous, partisan, occasionally pompous and sometimes undisguisedly playful, this was unquestionably Dr Johnson's Dictionary: 'Net—anything with interstitial vacuities'; 'Run—to ply the feet in such a manner as that both feet are at every step off the ground at the same time'; 'Lexicographer—a maker of dictionaries, a harmless drudge . . .'

Johnson's explosive aggressiveness has been ascribed to an underlying sense of inadequacy and insecurity. The massive chain that guarded the Gough Square front door may indicate a man less sure of himself than he sounded.

SAMUEL JOHNSON (1709–84)

GREGARIOUS, LONELY, AGGRESSIVE and physically grotesque, Johnson was forever the centre of any company and forever outside it. Between 1747 and 1759 this house was his stamping ground; he stamped it with unchallenged authority. It was in this building that he produced his Dictionary. Even with the help of the half-dozen scribes that he installed in the attic room ('The place looked like a counting house'), the job took eight years to complete.

When Boswell ventured to suggest that he had not realised what he was undertaking when he started it, Johnson was quick to correct him. 'Yes, Sir, I knew very well what I was undertaking—and very well how to do it—and have done it very well.'

He wrote other things during his twelve years here; there were his essays for *The Rambler* (every Tuesday and Saturday, twopence) but it was the Dictionary that kept him poor. A few months before moving in he had received an advance of £1,500 for the work. But this soon vanished.

He found himself often in debt. 'Sir,' said a letter to a Mr Richardson, 'I am obliged to entreat your assistance. I am under arrest for five pounds eighteen shillings. If you will be so good as to send me this sum I will very gratefully repay you and add it to all former obligations.' It was not the only letter of its kind that he had to write.

At home or at hostelries, Johnson invariably mixed meals and conversation. It was at the table at Gough Square that Mrs Thrale observed Johnson's extraordinary eating habits. 'Mr Johnson's pleasures—except those of conversation—are all coarse ones. He loves a good dinner dearly, eats it voraciously . . . Sauces his plum pudding with butter and pours sauce enough into every plate to drown all taste of the victuals.'

The finished dictionary contained 41,000 entries. It remained a standard work for more than a century. Each entry, illustrated with examples that Johnson had underlined in passages from his own reading in borrowed books, passed to the top floor for a long-hand transcription and insertion.

There was no doubt that Johnson was odd. He suffered, among other things, from stomach trouble, flatulence, catarrh, gout, asthma, dropsy. He had bad sight and bad hearing. There was doubt about his sexual stability. He drank tea obsessively—sometimes as many as sixteen cups at a sitting. His appetite was almost frightening; he gobbled his food 'so fast that the veins stood out on his forehead'. But when, in conversational company around the fire at Gough Square, he spoke—everyone listened carefully.

Underground Station:
CHANCERY LANE

'3 Durham Place' was built in 1794; the Bligh family were its first occupants. Bligh, forty when he moved in, had been at sea since the age of ten and had accompanied Captain Cook on his second expedition as master of the 'Resolution'. It had been five years earlier, on a voyage from the South Sea Islands to the West Indies, that mutiny had broken out aboard his ship the 'Bounty'. Bligh and eighteen of his crew were set adrift in an open boat by Fletcher Christian, the master's mate. Through Bligh's leadership, the party survived a 4,000-mile voyage, eventu-ally landing in the East Indies. The mutineers settled on Pitcairn Island; some of their descendants live there still. Bligh returned to England in 1790. He is buried close by at St Mary's, Lambeth.

WILLIAM BLIGH (1754–1817)

IT WAS DURING HIS TENANCY of this house that Bligh served at the battle of Copenhagen and was personally singled out for commendation by Nelson. But Bligh was a 'difficult' man; his career became better known for its downs than its ups.

Mrs Bligh's letter to her husband in Australia is one of the few documents that survive to throw light on the spirit of the house in Lambeth Road. Dated 11 August 1808 (the address at that time was 3 Durham Place), it indicates that, whatever might have been amiss with Captain Bligh abroad, there was little wrong at Lambeth North.

'My Dearest Love: I have this morning sent off a Box to Portsmouth for you, to go by the Spring Grove, a Ship of Mr Wilson's—in it are all letters from myself, your friends and the Dear children, all which I trust will give you pleasure. It likewise contains a Blue Cloath Coat with plain Buttons made by Collins—a Mixed Cloak and materials for making another which I think you will find useful for riding in,—3 pr of beautiful Silk Stocking—2 pr of Shoes by Staton and materials for 2 pr of Boots—2 pr of uniform Gloves—a Portrait of Fanny by Henry beautifully done, & all your newspapers & Magazines. It likewise contains for My Dear Mary 3 pr Silk Stocking—6 pr Gloves & 4 pr of Shoes. Inside some Music. These I think will be an intermediate supply until Brooks goes again. I wished Mr Wilson to have sent you some Liquors but he said Mr Campbell would let you have from the Cargo what you wanted & I was happy to hear that by a Ship of Mr Campbell's that went to Canton you had plentiful supplies of Tea, etc etc—this Box I hope you will receive safe with my most sincere and affectionate Love. The Dear Children again send their affectionate Duty—And I am My Dear Mr Bligh most sincerely your Elizabeth Bligh.'

Mrs Bligh did not know, as she wrote this letter, that her husband had once again seen mutiny—this time not as ship's captain but as Captain General and Governor of New South Wales. With his daughter and son-in-law he had sailed for Australia in February 1806—Bligh to take up his appointment and his son-in-law to serve as *aide de camp*. As it had done on the *Bounty*, Bligh's sense of discipline got the better of him; as before, he survived. By 1811 he was back at Lambeth—as a Rear-Admiral.

'Bligh was not an inhuman man,' says his biographer, Owen Rutter. *'There was a strong streak of affection in his make-up.'* But all the same he *'seems to have had the devilish knack of rolling off his tongue just those words that would be most wounding and would be remembered long after he had forgotten them . . .'* To his wife and family Bligh was loving-kindness itself: *'To you my love, I give all that an affectionate husband can give—love, respect & all that is or ever will be in the power of your ever affectionate Friend and Husband, Wm Bligh.'*

ADDITIONAL NOTABLE ADDRESSES

Names in brackets refer to nearest underground stations (except those asterisked, which indicate main line stations). Numerals (1m, 2m, etc) indicate distance in miles—as the crow flies—from Piccadilly Circus. The list is drawn largely from the comprehensive guide, 'Blue Plaques', published by the Greater London Council (10p). The Council's courtesy in making this abstract available is gratefully acknowledged. Further information will also be found in 'The Blue Plaque Guide' published by Newman Neame.

ARNOLD, Matthew *Poet and critic*
 2 Chester Square SW1   (Victoria)   1½m

BARRIE, Sir James *Novelist and dramatist*
 100 Bayswater Road W2   (Queensway)   2m

BARRY, Sir Charles *Architect*
 The Elms, Clapham Common North SW4
 (Clapham Common)   3½m

BEARDSLEY, Aubrey *Artist*
 114 Cambridge Street SW1   (Victoria)   2m

BEAUFORT, Sir Francis *Admiral and hydrographer*
 51 Manchester Street W1   (Baker Street)   1m

BEERBOHM, Sir Max *Artist and writer*
 57 Palace Gdns Terr W8   (Notting Hill Gate)   2½m

BELLOC, Hilaire *Author*
 104 Cheyne Walk SW3   (Sloane Square)   2½m

BENNETT, (Enoch) Arnold *Novelist*
 75 Cadogan Square SW1   (Sloane Square)   1½m

BESANT, Sir Walter *Novelist and antiquary*
 Frognal Gardens NW3   (Hampstead)   3½m

BORROW, George *Author*
 22 Hereford Square W2   (Gloucester Rd)   2½m

BROWNING, Elizabeth Barrett *Poet*
 99 Gloucester Place W1   (Baker Street)   1½m

BRUNEL, Sir Marc Isambard *Civil engineer*
 98 Cheyne Walk SW3   (Sloane Square)   2½m

BURGOYNE, General John
 10 Hertford Street W1   (Hyde Park Corner)   1m

BURKE, Edmund *Author and statesman*
 37 Gerrard Street W1   (Leicester Square)   ¼m

BURNEY, Fanny: Madame D'Arblay *Authoress*
 11 Bolton Street W1   (Green Park)   ½m

BUTT, Dame Clara *Singer*
 7 Harley Road NW3   (Swiss Cottage)   3m

CHAMBERLAIN, Joseph *Statesman*
 188 Camberwell Grove SE5   (Denmark Hill*)
 3½m

CHESTERTON, Gilbert Keith *Poet and novelist*
 11 Warwick Gdns W14   (West Kensington)   3½m

CHURCHILL, Winston *Statesman*
 28 Hyde Park Gate SW7   (High Street Kensington)   2½m

CLIVE of India, Lord *Soldier and administrator*
 45 Berkeley Square W1   (Green Park)   ¼m

COBDEN, Richard *Statesman*
 23 Suffolk Street SW1   (Piccadilly)   ¼m

COLERIDGE, Samuel Taylor *Poet and philosopher*
 7 Addisonbridge Pl W14   (West Kensington)   3½m

COLLINS, William Wilkie *Novelist*
 65 Gloucester Place W1   (Baker Street)   1½m

CONSTABLE, John *Painter*
 40 Well Walk NW3   (Hampstead)   3½m

CRANE, Walter *Artist*
 13 Holland St W8   (High Street Kensington)   3m

CRUIKSHANK, George *Artist*
 263 Hampstead Road NW1   (Mornington Crescent)   1½m

CUBITT, Thomas *Master builder*
 3 Lyall Street SW1   (Sloane Square)   1½m

DILKE, Sir Charles Wentworth *Statesman; author*
 76 Sloane Street SW1   (Sloane Square)   1½m

DRYDEN, John *Poet*
 43 Gerrard Street W1   (Leicester Square)   ¼m

DU MAURIER, George *Artist and writer*
 28 Hampstead Grove NW3   (Hampstead)   3½m

ELGAR, Sir Edward *Composer*
 51 Avonmore Rd W14   (West Kensington)   3½m

ENGELS, Friedrich *Socialist writer*
 141 Regent's Park Rd NW1   (Camden Town)   2½m

FOX, Charles James *Statesman*
 46 Clarges Street W1   (Green Park)   ¼m

FRIESE-GREENE, William *Cinematography pioneer*
 136 Maida Vale W9   (Kilburn Park)   3m

FUSELI, Henry *Artist*
 37 Foley Street W1   (Goodge Street)   1m

GALSWORTHY, John   *Novelist and playwright*
Grove Lodge, Hampstead Grove NW3
(Hampstead)   3½m

GALTON, Sir Francis   *Explorer; statistician*
42 Rutland Gate SW7   (Knightsbridge)   1½m

GANDHI, Mahatma   *Philosopher and teacher*
Kingsley Hall, Powis Road E3   (Bromley-by-
Bow)   6m

GASKELL, Mrs Elizabeth Cleghorn   *Novelist*
93 Cheyne Walk SW3   (Sloane Square)   2½m

GILBERT, Sir William Schwenck   *Dramatist*
39 Harrington Gdns SW7   (Gloucester Road)   2½m

GODWIN, George   *Architect, journalist and reformer*
24 Alexander Sq SW3   (South Kensington)   2½m

GOUNOD Charles   *Composer*
15 Morden Road SE3   (Blackheath*)   6½m

GRAHAME, Kenneth   *Author: 'Wind in the Willow's*
16 Phillimore Place W8   (High Street
Kensington)   3m

GREENAWAY, Kate   *Artist*
39 Frognal NW3   (Hampstead)   3½m

GROTE, George   *Historian*
12 Savile Row W1   (Piccadilly)   ¼m

HARDY, Thomas   *Poet and novelist*
172 Trinity Road SW17   (Tooting Bec)   5m

HENTY, George Alfred   *Author*
33 Lavender Gardens SW11   (Clapham
Common)   4m

HILL, Sir Rowland   *Postal reformer*
1 Orme Square W2   (Queensway)   2½m

HOLMAN-HUNT, William   *Painter*
18 Melbury Road W14   (High Street
Kensington)   3m

HOOD, Thomas   *Poet*
28 Finchley Road NW8   (St John's Wood)   2½m

HOUSMAN, A E   *Poet and scholar*
17 North Road N6   (Highgate)   5m

HOWARD, John   *Prison reformer*
23 Great Ormond St WC1   (Russell Square)   1m

HUNT, (James Henry) Leigh   *Essayist and poet*
22 Upper Cheyne Row SW3   (South
Kensington)   2½m

HUXLEY, Thomas Henry   *Biologist*
38 Marlborough Pl NW8   (St John's Wood)   2½m

IRVING, Sir Henry   *Actor*
15a Grafton Street W1   (Green Park)   ½m

JAMES, Henry   *Writer*
34 De Vere Gardens W8   (High Street
Kensington)   2½m

KITCHENER of Khartoum,   *Field Marshal*
2 Carlton Gdns SW1   (Trafalgar Square)   ¼m

KOSSUTH, Louis   *Hungarian patriot*
39 Chepstow Villas W11   (Nott Hill Gate)   3m

LAMB, Charles   *Essayist*
64 Duncan Terrace N1   (Angel)   2m

LAWRENCE, T E   *'Lawrence of Arabia'*
14 Barton Street SW1   (St James's Park)   1m

LIND, Jenny   *Singer*
189 Old Brompton Rd SW5   (Earls Court)   2½m

LUTYENS, Sir Edwin Landseer   *Architect*
13 Mansfield Street W1   (Oxford Circus)   1m

MANBY, Charles   *Civil Engineer*
60 Westbourne Terrace W2   (Royal Oak)   2½m

MAXIM, Sir Hiram   *Inventor and engineer*
57d Hatton Garden EC1   (Chancery Lane)   1m

MAXWELL, James Clerk   *Physicist*
16 Palace Gardens Terrace W8   (Notting Hill
Gate)   2½m

MAYHEW, Henry   *Founder of 'Punch' and author*
55 Albany St NW1   (Gt Portland Street)   1½m

MAZZINI, Giuseppe   *Italian patriot*
183 Gower Street NW1   (Warren Street)   1m

MEYNELL, Alice   *Poet and essayist*
47 Palace Court W2   (Queensway)   2½m

MILL, John Stuart   *Philosopher*
18 Kensington Square W8   (High Street
Kensington)   2½m

MILLAIS, Sir John Everett   *Painter*
2 Palace Gate W8   (High St Kensington)   2m

MORSE, Samuel   *American painter and inventor of
the Morse Code*
141 Cleveland St W1   (Gt Portland Street)   1m

MURRY, John Middleton   *Critic*
17 East Heath Road NW3   (Hampstead)   3½m

PAVLOVA, Anna   *Ballerina*
Ivy House, North End Road NW3   (Golders
Green)   5m

PINERO, Sir Arthur   *Playwright*
115a Harley Street W1   (Regent's Park)   1m

ROMNEY, George *Painter*
  Holly Bush Hill NW3 (Hampstead) 3½m

SHACKLETON, Sir Ernest (Henry) *Explorer*
  12 Westwood Hill SE26 (Sydenham*) 7m

SHERATON, Thomas *Furniture designer*
  163 Wardour Street W1 (Tottenham Court
  Road) ¼m

SHERIDAN, Richard Brinsley *Dramatist; statesman*
  14 Savile Row W1 (Piccadilly) ¼m

SMILES, Samuel *Author of 'Self Help*
  11 Granville Park SE13 (Lewisham*) 7m

STEER, Philip Wilson *Painter*
  109 Cheyne Walk SW10 (Sth Kensington) 2½m

SWINBURNE, Algernon Charles *Poet*
  11 Putney Hill SW15 (East Putney) 4½m

TAGORE, Rabindranath *Indian poet*
  3 Villas on the Heath, Vale of Health NW3
  (Hampstead) 3½m

TERRY, (Dame) Ellen *Actress*
  22 Barkston Gardens SW5 (Earls Court) 3m

THACKERAY, William Makepeace *Novelist*
  36 Onslow Square SW7 (Sth Kensington) 2½m

TREE, Sir Herbert Beerbohm *Actor-manager*
  31 Rosary Gdns SW7 (Gloucester Road) 2½m

WALPOLE, Sir Robert *Statesman*
  5 Arlington Street W1 (Green Park) ½m

WESLEY, John *Evangelist and founder of Methodism*
  47 City Road EC1 (Old Street) 2½m

WILBERFORCE, William *Opponent of Slavery*
  44 Cadogan Place SW1 (Sloane Square) 1½m

WOLFE, (General) James *Victor of Quebec*
  Macartney House (Greenwich Park) 7m

YEATS, William Butler *Poet and dramatist*
  23 Fitzroy Road NW1 (Chalk Farm) 3m

ZANGWILL, Israel *Writer and philanthropist*
  288 Old Ford Road E2 (Bethnal Green) 4m

ACKNOWLEDGEMENTS

Special thanks are due to Miss E D Mercer BA, FSA, Head Archivist of the Greater London Council, to Mr J F C Phillips BA, Curator of Maps and Prints, and to his predecessor, Mr V R Belcher, MA, for their help in the preparation of material for this book.

The author and publishers express their thanks to Mrs Enid Samuel, Mr Lance Sieveking, Mr Crispin Gill and Mr Brian Ash for their help with the section on H G Wells; to Lord Tennyson and the Director of Lincoln City Libraries for permission to reproduce the Edward Lear manuscript fragment from the Tennyson Research Centre Collection; to Miss Anna Freud for permission to photograph at Maresfield Gardens; to the Trustees of the British Museum for permission to reproduce Karl Marx's Reader's Ticket declaration; to the Hampstead Reference Library for permission to reproduce the fragment from John Keats' anatomical notebook; to the Victoria and Albert Museum for permission to reproduce the covers of 'Lady's World', 'Women's World', and the photograph of Charles Dickens' diary; to St Mary's Hospital, Paddington, for permission to photograph in Alexander Fleming's laboratory; to St Marylebone Reference Library for permission to reproduce the drawing of 48 Blandford Street and to the Trustees of the National Portrait Gallery for permission to reproduce many of the portraits.

Thanks are also due to Mrs Dorothy Bohm, De Groot Collis and Company, The 'Daily Telegraph', The Dickens Fellowship, Mr John Dudman, The Fitzroy Collection, Guy's Hospital, International Students Trust, Mrs Johanna Harrison, Jaeger Limited, The John Lewis Partnership, Mr Ronald Julyan, Mr Michael Howard, The London School of Economics, Marconi Company Limited, The Royal College of General Practitioners, The Royal Society of Arts, United States Information Office and St Marylebone Public Library.